CHARACTER Counts

Build a Life
That Pleases God

From the Bible-Teaching Ministry of
CHARLES R. SWINDOLL

INSIGHT FOR LIVING

Charles R. Swindoll graduated in 1963 from Dallas Theological Seminary, where he now serves as the school's fourth president, helping to prepare a new generation of men and women for the ministry. Chuck has served in pastorates in three states: Massachusetts, Texas, and California, including almost twenty-three years at the First Evangelical Free Church in Fullerton, California. He is currently senior pastor of Stonebriar Community Church in Frisco, Texas, north of Dallas. His sermon messages have been aired over radio since 1979 as the *Insight for Living* broadcast. A best-selling author, he has written numerous books and booklets on many subjects.

Based on the outlines and transcripts of Charles. R. Swindoll's sermons, in 1993 the Bible study guide titled *Building Blocks of Biblical Character* was coauthored by Bryce Klabunde, a graduate of Biola University and Dallas Theological Seminary. In 2000 this guide was reprinted under the new title *Character Counts*.

Editor in Chief:
Cynthia Swindoll

Coauthor of Text:
Bryce Klabunde

Assistant Editor:
Wendy Peterson

Copy Editors:
Deborah Gibbs
Cheryl Gilmore
Karene Wells

Rights and Permissions:
The Meredith Agency

Graphic System Administrator:
Bob Haskins

Director, Communications Division:
John Norton

Print Production Manager:
Don Bernstein

Print Buyer:
Becki Sue Gómez

Unless otherwise identified, all Scripture references are from the New American Standard Bible, © The Lockman Foundation 1960, 1962, 1963, 1968, 1971, 1972, 1973, 1975, 1977, 1995. Used by permission.

Scripture taken from the Holy Bible, New International Version, Copyright © 1973, 1978, 1984 International Bible Society, used by permission of Zondervan Bible Publishers.

An effort has been made to locate sources and obtain permission where necessary for the quotations used in this book. In the event of any unintentional omission, a modification will gladly be incorporated in future printings.

ISBN 1-57972-361-6
Cover design: Michael Standlee Design
Cover image: © 2000 Index Stock Imagery/Jim Mcguire
Printed in the United States of America

CONTENTS

INTRODUCTION

There are few things more important to talk about today than character. I can honestly say that almost every day of my life I think of developing it in myself and my four children. I still look for books that I want us to read on character. I still talk about films I've seen that develop character. I want one thing for them more than anything else: character, greatness of character!

And I want that for you as well.

Receiving Jesus Christ is basic to this pursuit, but that's not the end of the story. He comes and gives power and grace, but He doesn't automatically bring character. That's your move.

In this series, we'll carve out of God's Word a few building blocks of character that you can fit into your life. One by one, set them in place, and erect a sturdy pillar of character that will stand the test of time.

Chuck Swindoll

Chuck Swindoll

PUTTING TRUTH
INTO ACTION

K nowledge apart from application falls short of God's desire for His children. He wants us to apply what we learn so that we will change and grow. This study guide was prepared with these goals in mind. As you go through the following pages, we hope your desire to discover biblical truth will grow as your understanding of God's Word increases and that you will be encouraged to apply what you've learned.

To assist you in your study, we've included a section called **Living Insights** at the end of each lesson. These exercises will challenge you to study further and to think of specific ways to put your discoveries into action.

On occasion a lesson is followed by a **Digging Deeper** section, which gives you additional information and resources to probe further into some issues raised in that lesson.

There are many ways to use this guide—in personal devotions, group studies, discussions with friends and family, and Sunday School classes. And, of course, it's an ideal study aid when you're listening to its corresponding *Insight for Living* radio series.

To benefit most from this study guide, we would encourage you to consider it a spiritual journal. That's why we've included space in the **Living Insights** for recording your thoughts and discoveries. We hope you'll return to those sections often for review and encouragement as you continue to grow in your walk with Christ.

Insight for Living

**Build a Life
That Pleases God**

Chapter 1

THEY, BEING DEAD, STILL SPEAK

Hebrews 11:32–38

Who speaks for you when hard times call? Friends may stand with you or hold your hand. They may speak to you with words of courage and truth. But can they speak *for* you? In the midst of a trial, when the pressure squeezes you from all sides, only your character can testify on your behalf. By *character*, we mean your moral, ethical, and spiritual undergirding that

❑ rests on truth,

❑ reinforces a life,

❑ resists the temptation to compromise.

Remember when Jesus stood beneath the stark light of the high priest's glare? No one spoke for Him. Like a meek lamb, He faced His accusers silently and alone. What did speak on His behalf that day, however, was His magnificent character—the lion in the shadows.

Think of the people who have influenced you with the silent strength of their character—perhaps a teacher, a coach, a parent, a neighbor, or a pastor. You may recall the times their integrity and ideals spoke for them during hardships. In many ways, they were the ones who set the mold into which you have poured your own life. What building blocks did these people use to construct their moral excellence? And how can we carve out these same blocks to use in our lives? To begin answering these questions, let's make a few initial observations about those who leave us a lasting legacy of character greatness.

The Lasting Legacy of Character Greatness

First, *greatness of character is found only in people.* Of all God's

1

creation, only humans bear the stamp of His image—a stamp that separates us from the animal world and gives us a built-in moral capacity (see Gen. 1:26–27). Into that character reservoir God pours glimpses of His own character in such forms as justice, honesty, and virtue. Consequently, as the saying goes, "If you would understand virtue, observe the conduct of virtuous people." We will not discover virtue in nature, neither can we find it in technology or material wealth. Character is a product of the human soul, as God intended.

Second, *it is developed and proven in the crucibles of pain and difficulty.* Have you ever known anyone with character who was not well acquainted with pain? The reason is that hardship, not comfort, tempers strong character.[1]

Perhaps you're feeling the heat of the crucible right now—your business is riding a rocky path or your marriage is floundering in a storm of stress. Maybe a false accusation has blackened your clean reputation or a physical ailment has thrown you into confusion and fear. Can any good emerge from these difficulties? The apostle Paul was able to exult in his trials,

> knowing that tribulation brings about perseverance; and perseverance, proven character; and proven character, hope; and hope does not disappoint, because the love of God has been poured out within our hearts through the Holy Spirit who was given to us. (Rom. 5:3b–5)

Naturally, we tend to run from pain as soon as it strikes. But can we really escape to some hidden island where adversities will not find us? No, as one of Job's counselors observed, "For man is born for trouble, As sparks fly upward" (Job 5:7).[2] There is no golden ticket to a trouble-free life.

---

1. For centuries, philosophers have recognized this truth. Seneca said, "It is a rough road that leads to the heights of greatness." According to Goethe, "A talent is formed in stillness, a character in the world's torrent." And Stendhal wisely added, "One can acquire everything in solitude—except character." As quoted in *Bartlett's Familiar Quotations,* 15th ed., rev. and enl., ed. Emily Morison Beck (Boston, Mass.: Little, Brown and Co., 1980), pp. 114, 395, 453.

2. Highlighting pain's role as a deliberate part of God's plan, commentator Franz Delitzsch explained the passage this way: "Misfortune does not grow out of the ground like weeds; it is rather established in the divine order of the world, as it is established in the order of nature that sparks of fire should ascend." From *Job,* vol. 4 of *Commentary on the Old Testament in Ten Volumes,* by C. F. Keil and F. Delitzsch (reprint; Grand Rapids, Mich.: William B. Eerdmans Publishing Co., 1978), vol. 1 of 2 vols. in 1, p. 99.

Rather than escaping, the better plan is to meet hardship head-on. Resist the temptations to feel sorry for yourself or to blame others. Cooperate with pain, and as Paul taught, let it follow its course in your life all the way to "proven character." Jesus Himself is our model, for

> although He was a Son, He learned obedience from
> the things which He suffered. (Heb. 5:8)

Third, *it is not quickly acquired.* Great character is not a mail-order commodity, shipped by overnight express. We can't expect it to arrive at our doorstep, neatly packaged with no assembly required. It does not come to us that easily, nor does it happen inside us automatically or by accident. It takes time . . . and individual effort.

Being raised by good parents may start you in the right direction, but at some point, each person must take the reins of responsibility for his or her own character development. Anne Frank, who journalized her feelings in a diary while hiding from the Nazis during World War II, came to understand this truth.

> [Daddy] said: "All children must look after their
> own upbringing." Parents can only give good advice
> or put them on the right paths, but the final forming
> of a person's character lies in their own hands.[3]

Fourth, *it is not necessarily a permanent possession.* Falling like petals from the pages of your Bible are the stories of many godly men and women whose vibrant character wilted away. The reasons for their lapses are varied—moral compromise, greed, fear, stress. But the results are the same: embarrassment, loss of respect, and wasted potential.

That's why it's so important, especially in today's dry moral climate, to till God's values into the soil during our children's formative years. The day will come, sooner than we imagine, for them to grow their own character. Will their moral roots be deep enough to last a lifetime?

For our children's sake—and for our sake—we must emphasize character development. Teachers, don't merely stuff your students' minds with facts and figures; coaches, don't just drive your players to be a winning team. Build character! Those who work with the

---

3. Anne Frank, as quoted in *Bartlett's Familiar Quotations*, p. 909.

public, don't rely on wardrobe and words more than inner moral fiber. Remember: who we are is more significant than how we look. Integrity and courage are more important than image and position.

But these days, where can we find people who model these ideals? Usually not on the pages of the daily newspaper. A better place to look is the Bible; specifically, the spiritual memorial in Hebrews 11.

A List of Lives worth Honoring

When we enter Hebrews 11, we are walking into the hush of a burial ground, with these verses the stone-etched epitaphs. Avoid trying to analyze them for any doctrinal secrets. Rather, absorb the stories with your soul. Let those who are dead still speak to you, person to person.

Names to Remember . . . and Why

Many familiar names mark the gravestones that line the path through this chapter. They read: Abel, Enoch, and Noah; Abraham and Sarah; their son Isaac and his son and grandson, Jacob and Joseph. There's Moses, the reluctant deliverer, and Rahab, the harlot. Every single one of these people was imperfect—just like us. Yet each one exhibited greatness of character.

Perhaps you've thought that past failures in your life have disqualified you from God's character race. If so, consider Moses, who murdered an Egyptian taskmaster, or Rahab, who was a prostitute. If they could put their pasts behind them and go on to win the race, so can you.

In verse 32, more markers line the memorial path:

> And what more shall I say? For time will fail me
> if I tell of Gideon, Barak, Samson, Jephthah, of
> David and Samuel and the prophets.

At this point, the writer realizes the list of names could go on and on. The cemetery is full of gravestones with epitaphs—stories of faith that model greatness of character through both triumphs and tragedies. Here are a few of the amazing triumphs these men and women of honor accomplished:

> By faith [they] conquered kingdoms, performed acts
> of righteousness, obtained promises, shut the mouths
> of lions, quenched the power of fire, escaped the

edge of the sword, from weakness were made strong, became mighty in war, put foreign armies to flight. Women received back their dead by resurrection. (vv. 33–35a)

In the next verses the tone of the passage shifts to a minor key, with tragedy eclipsing the sunlight of victory.

Others were tortured, not accepting their release, so that they might obtain a better resurrection; and others experienced mockings and scourgings, yes, also chains and imprisonment. They were stoned, they were sawn in two, they were tempted, they were put to death with the sword; they went about in sheepskins, in goatskins, being destitute, afflicted, ill-treated (men of whom the world was not worthy), wandering in deserts and mountains and caves and holes in the ground. (vv. 35b–38)

We weep over these epitaphs and shudder at the images of torment our minds conjure up. Yet rising from the graves that hold these maimed and broken bodies is a fragrance of faith that inspires us during our own personal triumphs and tragedies. As a result, we leave the cemetery determined to follow in their footsteps, wherever they may lead.

Traits to Repeat . . . and How

The writer to the Hebrews says rightly that these were men and women "of whom the world was not worthy" (v. 38a). Could the same be said of us? If we take our cues from the secular world and the famous people whose images flicker on our television screens, we'll never achieve the goal. Virtue and integrity are godly qualities beyond this world's understanding. By aspiring to have them for ourselves, we have to let go of our desire for popularity. And we have to begin being true to ourselves as we answer to God. Even if the world misunderstands us, we need to keep doing what we know God wants us to do.

Some Easily Forgotten Reminders about Character

If you choose to follow those in Hebrews 11, here are some helpful traveling tips. First, *character tends to flourish in later life when good seeds are planted in early life.* Train your children and grandchildren

5

when they are young. Teach them that good character is what truly matters in life, even more than good grades or a good win-loss record in sports.

Second, *character seems more possible in us when we see it modeled in others.* The best mentor is not a how-to book or a technique but a life. Become a student of great people. Read biographies. Choose your heroes like you would choose your closest friends.

Third, *character can withstand the hard times if it is cultivated during the days of ease.* Since it is difficult to lay a foundation in the rain, don't wait until the storms of testing arrive to fortify your character. The best time to build is while the sun is still shining.

Living Insights

Like the coal smoke that billowed from the tenement chimneys, a moral blackness had settled on the city of London by the year 1787. Emerging from the soot was an empire built on the backs of the illiterate poor. Dickensian children worked the mines and mills, eighteen hours a day, for a few shillings a month. Slave traders plowed the high seas to Africa, harvesting human flesh and supplying it to the West Indian plantations. Back home, the pampered rich hoarded their bounty of cash for private pleasures, not caring that the coins themselves were tainted with the blood of human suffering.

In the midst of this blackness stood one young Christian, just coming to full height in his faith—William Wilberforce. Not yet thirty years old, Wilberforce was already a political veteran, having won the coveted Yorkshire seat, the most powerful constituency, in the House of Commons. A small man, barely five feet tall, he would become the David to fight the immoral Goliaths of his society.

"The Lord has raised you up to the good of His church and for the good of the nation," the forceful clergyman John Newton told him one day. As Wilberforce pondered what that might mean, the plight of African men and women herded like beasts into the bellies of slave ships came to his attention. He was appalled that London's decadent lifestyle was financed by this atrocity. On a foggy Sunday morning in 1787, he penned in his journal: "Almighty God has set before me two great objectives. The abolition of the slave trade and the reformation of [morals]."

Focusing his passion on these goals, Wilberforce joined forces with fellow abolitionists and began collecting the stones of evidence they would need to do battle. The first encounter in 1788 proved successful with the passage of a bill that limited the number of slaves who could be transported per ship. This victory, however, inflamed the corrupt bloc of legislators kept in office by the powerful traders. Subsequent attempts to abolish slave trading met furious opposition.

In 1791, Wilberforce, the "dwarf with big resounding name" as he was mocked in a poem, mounted a well-prepared assault, blasting the slave trade with booming eloquence. The opposition asserted that abolition would put thousands of sailors out of work, destroy the lucrative West Indies trade, and cripple the economy. In the end, "commerce clinked its purse," as one person observed, and Wilberforce lost.

But he did not give up. Again and again, he pleaded the case of the abused African. In 1792, he and his abolitionist friends took their cause to the common people, using as an emblem the picture of a slave pleading: "Am I not a man and a brother?" A boycott of slave-grown sugar was organized, petitions were filed . . . but the powerful West Indian bloc still defeated the legislation.

Behind the scenes, he and his companions kept working, forming the Society for the Education of Africans, the Society for Bettering the Condition of the Poor, and other organizations to bring light to London's moral darkness. In the meantime, Wilberforce continued to present his bills against the slave trade despite failure every time.

Finally, after twenty years of tireless effort, at four o'clock in the morning on February 4, 1807, the bill to abolish the slave trade passed. Later in the month, when the Parliament ratified the legislation, members of the House cheered Wilberforce's passionate labors. Tears of relief and joy streamed down his face as he realized the battle was won at last.

The Goliath slave trade was dead, but there were other giants to overcome. Total freedom for existing slaves was Wilberforce's next vision—a dream that eventually came true three days before his death in 1833, when Parliament passed the Bill for the Abolition of Slavery.

William Wilberforce was a man of great character. More concerned with justice and righteousness than political popularity, he risked all to stand for what was right. In many ways, his stand led to the abolition of slavery in the United States thirty years later, when Abraham Lincoln freed the slaves in 1863. Displaced Africans all around the world can trace their liberty to William Wilberforce and his thundering voice of freedom.[4]

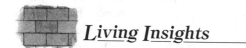

Living Insights

Do you think clouds of discouragement ever shrouded Wilberforce's soul? According to Charles Colson and Ellen Santilli Vaughn,

> Weary with grief and frustration, he often sat long into the night at his old oak desk, wondering whether he should abandon his hopeless campaign.[5]

Twenty years is a long time to keep losing the same battle. Perhaps you've been fighting for what is right within your community, your family, or within yourself. Have you felt like giving up? If so, take a moment to describe your battle and your feelings.

Read Romans 8:31–39 and Galatians 6:7–10. Then listen to a friend's exhortation to Wilberforce based on these verses.

> Unless God has raised you up for this very thing, you will be worn out by the opposition of men and devils, but if God be for you who can be against you? Are all of them together stronger than God? Oh, be not weary of well-doing. Go on in the name of God, and in the power of His might, till even American slavery, the vilest that ever saw the sun, shall vanish away before it. That He that has guided you from

4. William Wilberforce's story is based on chapter 8 of *Kingdoms in Conflict*, by Charles Colson with Ellen Santilli Vaughn (New York, N.Y.: William Morrow; Grand Rapids, Mich.: Zondervan Publishing House, 1987), pp. 95–108.

5. Colson and Vaughn, *Kingdoms in Conflict*, p. 104.

8

your youth up may continue to strengthen in this and all things, is the prayer of,

Your affectionate servant,
John Wesley[6]

In the following space, express your confidence in Him who is for you. Commit to Him your battle, and pray for His strength.

_____

_____

_____

_____

_____

_____

_____

6. Colson and Vaughn, *Kingdoms in Conflict*, p. 105.

Chapter 2

THE DISCERNMENT
OF ABIGAIL

1 Samuel 25:1–42

With so many men and women of great character in Scripture, whom should we select as our models?

We could choose any of the people listed in the Hebrews 11 hall of faith: Abraham, Sarah, Jacob, Joseph, and all the rest who sparkle in Scripture's sky as beacons of integrity. But let's take a different approach. Let's look to some lesser lights on the biblical horizon, whose character fueled the fire of the more famous. Let's uncover some hidden heroes, without whose inspiration the greater lights might have faded away. Let's look for the people behind the celebrities . . . as in David's case, a discerning woman named Abigail.

A Little Background, Please

To set the scene for Abigail's story, a little background information is in order. David has been anointed king by the prophet Samuel, but his rightful crown still sits firmly on the brow of defiant King Saul—his jealous adversary. At the top of Saul's most-wanted list, David has been running for his life, moving from hideout to hideout. Accompanying him is an odd mix of people: "everyone who was in distress, and everyone who was in debt, and everyone who was discontented" (1 Sam. 22:2). Together, though, they have become an efficient army of about six hundred men (23:13).

David leads his band of nomads to the wilderness of Paran, where they hope to scratch out a living by policing the area for the local ranchers. Although no contracts are signed—a custom of the day—they work hard protecting the herds of sheep from thieves and wild animals. At shearing time, the rich ranchers gather the herds to shave off their profits. Customarily, it is also the time when the owners remunerate the volunteer police for their services. Only a tightfisted miser would refuse to pay.

Parts of this chapter are based on "The Woman Who Saved Her Husband's Neck," from the study guide *Memorable Scenes from Old Testament Homes*, written by Bryce Klabunde, from the Bible-teaching ministry of Charles R. Swindoll (Anaheim, Calif.: Insight for Living, 1992).

Like Nabal, the villain in our drama.

Let's Meet the Main Characters

Let's take a moment to acquaint ourselves with this ancient Scrooge and the two other main characters of our story.

Nabal

> Now there was a man in Maon whose business was in Carmel; and the man was very rich, and he had three thousand sheep and a thousand goats. . . . But the man was harsh and evil in his dealings.[1] (25:2a, 3b)

Wealthy Nabal's infamy, like his vast herd, has spread throughout the countryside. His own servants complain that "he is such a worthless man that no one can speak to him" (v. 17b). Even his name betrays his mulish character—it means "fool." According to Alfred Edersheim, this was

> an ominous designation in Old Testament parlance, where "the fool" represented the headstrong, self-willed person, who followed his own course, as if there were "no God" alike in heaven and on earth.[2]

That's Nabal. Self-willed. Greedy. Angry. Such a man, we might think, is probably married to an equally ill-natured, Jezebel-type woman. Actually, Nabal's wife is very much the opposite.

Abigail

> Now the man's name was Nabal, and his wife's name was Abigail. And the woman was intelligent and beautiful in appearance. (v. 3a)

Abigail is as wise as Nabal is foolish.[3] She possesses, as we'll see

---

1. The Hebrew word for *harsh* is *qasheh*, meaning "hard, severe, rough, or rude." At times, it is translated "stubborn" (Judg. 2:19), "obstinate" (Isa. 48:4), and "cruel" (19:4).

2. Alfred Edersheim, *Israel under Samuel, Saul, and David, to the Birth of Solomon*, vol. 1 of *The Bible History: Old Testament* (1890; reprint, Grand Rapids, Mich.: William B. Eerdmans Publishing Co., 1949), vol. 4 of 4 vols. in 1, p. 129.

3. How did Abigail and Nabal wind up married to each other? Their marriage was probably arranged by their parents. Although this custom sometimes works out well, in Abigail's case it was disastrous. Still, despite her churlish husband, this remarkable woman retained her dignity.

in the story, the rare quality of discernment—the ability to read people and situations and act according to what is best. This requires not only intelligence but also goodness. A discerning person must be approachable, realistic, well-organized, and trustworthy. All of these traits grow out of Abigail's character and blossom in her striking beauty.

David

Then there's David, who is living with his followers in tents on the barren, sun-baked hillsides of Paran. This is not the kingly life he imagined when Samuel's oil of blessing trickled down his neck. He's dirty. He's tired. And, according to his own words, he feels like a hunted animal (see Ps. 57:4–6).

When you mix Nabal's flaming selfishness with David's short fuse of frustration . . . need we say what might happen if the two of them got together?

Natural Conflicts . . . Discerning Solutions

Actually, two confrontations could erupt in this story. The first possibility involves Nabal and Abigail.

Husband-Wife Conflict

Imagine Abigail's life with her boorish husband. Two people couldn't be more opposite. He reacts with prideful emotion; she responds with God-centered discernment. He thinks only of himself; she considers everyone involved. How she must cringe inside when he stalks around the house on a tirade. Yet, fortunately for Nabal, she stays with him in spite of their differences.

Employee-Employer Conflict

What happens instead—the conflict we've been building up to—occurs between David and Nabal. As we mentioned earlier, it is shearing time on Nabal's ranch, so David sends ten emissaries to remind Nabal of their service and to collect the well-deserved gratuity (1 Sam. 25:4–5). He doesn't even ask for a certain amount; instead, he graciously leaves the payment up to the landowner and sends along this blessing:

> "'Have a long life, peace be to you, and peace be to
> your house, and peace be to all that you have. . . .

Please give whatever you find at hand to your servants and to your son David.'" (vv. 6, 8b)

Having relayed these words to Nabal, the ten men politely wait for his response (v. 9). In no way do they threaten him or demand money, wool, or mutton. Yet Nabal replies sarcastically:

"Who is David? And who is the son of Jesse? There are many servants today who are each breaking away from his master. Shall I then take my bread and my water and my meat that I have slaughtered for my shearers, and give it to men whose origin I do not know?" (vv. 10b–11)

Nabal thinks nothing of snubbing the Lord's anointed and, with a wave of his hand, shoos the men away. They must now return to their leader empty-handed.

As they shuffle back into camp, we can imagine that David has already fired up the barbecue and is licking his lips in anticipation of his long-awaited rack-of-lamb feast. "Well, where's the pay? No pay? No wool? No meat!" Slowly, they recount Nabal's insults. David's short fuse is lit, and in a blast of anger, the king-in-waiting throws aside his godly mantle and cries out to his men, "Each of you gird on his sword" (v. 13a). Spewing bitterness and revenge, he vows:

"Surely in vain I have guarded all that this man has in the wilderness, so that nothing was missed of all that belonged to him; and he has returned me evil for good. May God do so to the enemies of David, and more also, if by morning I leave as much as one male of any who belong to him." (vv. 21–22)

Meanwhile, back at the ranch, Abigail finds out from a loyal servant about Nabal's foolish rebuff of David's men.

"Behold, David sent messengers from the wilderness to greet our master, and he scorned them. Yet the men were very good to us. . . . They were a wall to us both by night and by day, all the time we were with them tending the sheep. Now therefore, know and consider what you should do, for evil is plotted against our master and against all his household; and

13

he is such a worthless man that no one can speak
to him." (vv. 14b–15a, 16–17)

Abigail does not have to "consider" long for she knows what
she has to do. She may have been tempted to think, "My, but God
works in mysterious ways! Let's pray that my dear husband's passing
will be swift and painless." But instead, she wisely considers the
painful consequences of David's rash act, not only for her "worthless" husband but also for David, whose reputation as the soon-to-
be king needs protecting. So, without Nabal's knowing it, she puts
her plan into action.

First, she whips up a feast for David and his men (v. 18). Then
she rides off to intercept them in the hills (vv. 19–20). Thundering
across the desert are David and four hundred of his men—their
faces steeled for battle, their swords set for blood (v. 13). Coura-
geously, Abigail approaches them, defended only by the disarming
aroma of the food wafting in the breeze.

Observe the diplomacy of Abigail. She first employs *tact*. In her
speech, she will call herself "your maidservant" six times and call
David "my lord" fourteen times. She understands protocol.

Second, she expresses *humility* by interceding on behalf of her
husband yet not excusing Nabal's foolishness.

> When Abigail saw David, she hurried and dis-
> mounted from her donkey, and fell on her face before
> David, and bowed herself to the ground. She fell at
> his feet and said, "On me alone, my lord, be the
> blame. And please let your maidservant speak to
> you, and listen to the words of your maidservant.
> Please do not let my lord pay attention to this worth-
> less man, Nabal, for as his name is, so is he. Nabal
> is his name and folly is with him; but I your maid-
> servant did not see the young men of my lord whom
> you sent." (vv. 23–25)

Third, with her gift in hand, she affirms her *loyalty* to David
and to his best interests. And fourth, she illustrates her *faith* in God.
Her eyes are on David's future as the next king of Israel—a future
that would be jeopardized by this act of vengeance.

> "Please forgive the transgression of your maidser-
> vant; for the Lord will certainly make for my lord
> an enduring house, because my lord is fighting the

battles of the Lord, and evil shall not be found in you all your days. . . . And when the Lord does for my lord according to all the good that He has spoken concerning you, and appoints you ruler over Israel, this will not cause grief or a troubled heart to my lord, both by having shed blood without cause and by my lord having avenged himself. When the Lord deals well with my lord, then remember your maidservant." (vv. 28, 30–31)

With each word, David's heart softens. Finally, more in keeping with his characteristic humility, David submits to what he knows is the truth, relieved that someone had the discernment to stop him at the threshold of a terrible mistake.

Then David said to Abigail, "Blessed be the Lord God of Israel, who sent you this day to meet me, and blessed be your discernment, and blessed be you, who have kept me this day from bloodshed, and from avenging myself by my own hand. Nevertheless, as the Lord God of Israel lives, who has restrained me from harming you, unless you had come quickly to meet me, surely there would not have been left to Nabal until the morning light as much as one male." So David received from her hand what she had brought him and said to her, "Go up to your house in peace. See, I have listened to you and granted your request." (vv. 32–35)

Whew! Her work done, Abigail turns for home . . . and Nabal.

Then Abigail came to Nabal, and behold, he was holding a feast in his house, like the feast of a king. And Nabal's heart was merry within him, for he was very drunk; so she did not tell him anything at all until the morning light. (v. 36)

This ungrateful drunk is the man whose neck she just saved! She knows she will receive no word of thanks from him, so she goes to sleep trusting God for her reward—which comes unexpectedly the next morning.

But in the morning, when the wine had gone out of Nabal, his wife told him these things, and his heart died within him so that he became as a stone. About ten days later, the Lord struck Nabal, and he died. (vv. 37–38)

The Lord Himself vindicates Abigail and David. But the story's not over.

A Pleasant Ending, Well-Deserved

When David heard that Nabal was dead, he said, "Blessed be the Lord, who has pleaded the cause of my reproach from the hand of Nabal and has kept back His servant from evil. The Lord has also returned the evildoing of Nabal on his own head." Then David sent a proposal to Abigail, to take her as his wife. (v. 39)

And Abigail wastes no time in accepting David's proposal of marriage (v. 42). A romantic end to one woman's story of courage and grace.

Regarding the Value of Discernment

Abigail may be one of Scripture's lesser lights, yet were it not for her illuminating character, David's greater light might have dimmed forever. While her qualities still glow in our minds, let's reflect on a couple of principles regarding the value of discernment.

First, *when there is discernment, there need not be a great display of strength.* A soft touch on the wrist or a timely word spoken in love is powerful enough to prevent the most foolish of actions. Abigail's story is proof that gentle answers—not fiery debates or manipulative tactics—truly do turn away wrath (see Prov. 15:1).

Second, *when there is discernment, wisdom is rewarded with relief from above.* David proclaimed:

I waited patiently for the Lord;
And He inclined to me, and heard my cry.
He brought me up out of the pit of destruction, out
of the miry clay;
And He set my feet upon a rock making my
footsteps firm. (Ps. 40:1–2)

At this moment, you may have every right to even the score with someone who has harmed you. But, with the Lord's strength, resist that urge. Let Him draw you out of the pit of destruction and set your feet on the solid ground of discernment.

Living Insights

Look inside your heart's vest pocket. Are you carrying with you a little book of revenge? Most of us keep one handy so that when someone wrongs us, we can stick that offense like a trading stamp on the pages of the book. Collect enough stamps, and . . .

Take the average married couple, for instance. The husband says something insensitive; the wife puts a stamp in her book. The husband watches television rather than listening to her; she pastes a row of stamps in the book. He tells an embarrassing story about her in front of his friends; she slaps a whole page of stamps in her book. This goes on and on. Then one afternoon he says something sarcastic to her—a harmless remark to him. Boom! She explodes. Fire flashes in her eyes, her body tenses, her jaw clinches, and out pours a Niagara of caustic words that sends him reeling.

"What did I say? What did I do?" he pleads stupidly. It's *everything* he said and *everything* he did. She has it all in stamps. And today she has redeemed her book for a delicious dose of revenge.[4]

How full is your book? Are you getting close to cashing it in for some revenge? Whose names are on the stamps? What have they done?

_____

_____

_____

Step back for a moment and take a few deep breaths. Feel a little calmer now? Then let's try to gain some perspective on stamp saving. How important to you are these people, these relationships? Are they worth more than your revenge?

Scripture says,

> Never take your own revenge, beloved, but leave room
> for the wrath of God, for it is written, "Vengeance

4. Adapted from H. Norman Wright in *Communication: Key to Your Marriage* (Ventura, Calif.: Regal Books, GL Publications, 1974), pp. 141–43.

is Mine, I will repay," says the Lord. (Rom. 12:19)

Can we be your Abigail for a moment? The Lord has great plans for you. Would you destroy them through bitterness? Vengeance is the Lord's concern. Please, won't you give Him your book?

 ## *Living Insights* STUDY TWO

Abigail characterizes discernment . . . and so much more.

According to *Merriam-Webster's*, *discernment* means "the quality of being able to grasp and comprehend what is obscure."[5] That's one nuance. Let's read further for related words that describe more of Abigail's character:

> *Discrimination* stresses the power to distinguish and select what is true or appropriate or excellent; *perception* implies quick and often sympathetic discernment (as of shades of feeling); *penetration* implies a searching mind that goes beyond what is obvious or superficial; *insight* suggests depth of discernment coupled with understanding sympathy; *acumen* implies characteristic penetration combined with keen practical judgment.[6]

Now that's Abigail! In which of these qualities do you excel?

_____

_____

_____

In what ways do you wish you could be more like Abigail?

_____

_____

_____

5. *Merriam-Webster's Collegiate Dictionary*, 10th ed., see "discernment."
6. *Merriam-Webster's*, see synonyms listed under "discernment."

Perhaps someone you know is like David: on a collision course with disaster. As you review the qualities of discernment—discrimination, perception, penetration, insight, acumen—which ones can you use to help this person?

_____

_____

_____

_____

It also takes courage to be an Abigail. Don't hesitate. Your friend needs a soft touch on the wrist—something you can give.

Chapter 3

THE REFRESHMENT
OF ONESIPHORUS

2 Timothy 1:15–18

> **WANTED:** Refreshing person.
> Education required: None.
> Experience needed: None.
> Qualifications: Must sense
> hidden needs; must love
> without expectations; must
> encourage.
> *Flatterers need not apply.*

Do you have a friend who could qualify for this position? A friend who genuinely cares, whose words are uplifting and not judgmental, whose presence is like a refreshing spring shower?

You're fortunate if you do, for all around us are people who plod through life as through a desert, hoping someone will quench their parched spirits with a cool cup of encouragement. Actress Celeste Holm said, "We live by encouragement and die without it—slowly, sadly and angrily."[1] How tragic is the life without human refreshment.

Our world needs Christians who are involved in the spiritual ministry of refreshment.[2] Perhaps you would like to apply for this position yourself. What kind of character qualities does it require? If we asked the apostle Paul, he would describe the qualities of his dear friend Onesiphorus. Like Abigail, Onesiphorus may be unknown to us; but to Paul, in the middle of his arid wasteland of loneliness, Onesiphorus was a lush oasis of hope. Let's get to know this encouraging man from Paul's portrait of him in 2 Timothy 1.

Some Background Information

To fully appreciate Paul's relationship with Onesiphorus, it's

---

1. Celeste Holm, as quoted in *The Reader's Digest Treasury of Modern Quotations* (New York, N.Y.: Reader's Digest Press, 1975), p. 484.

2. A spiritual ministry is different from a spiritual gift. The Holy Spirit distributes at least one spiritual gift to all believers, but not all believers have all the gifts. However, spiritual ministries—such as love, forgiveness, compassion, and hospitality—apply to all of God's children (compare Rom. 12:4–8 with vv. 9–21).

important for us to get a handle on some background information—in particular, where Paul is when he writes his second letter to Timothy.

Where Paul Is

The apostle is in prison, but not just any prison. According to biographer John Pollock,

> He was among the felons in the Mamertine or an equally obnoxious dungeon, reached only by rope or ladder let through a hole in the floor above. His weary body must lie on rough stones. The air was foul, sanitation almost nonexistent.[3]

It is here Paul will spend his final days on earth.

How Paul Feels

With his life's work concluding and death creeping closer every day, Paul probably feels a bit nostalgic. Faces and names from his past occupy his time now—how he wishes some of those friends could be with him! For blowing through this cold dungeon is a draft of loneliness that chills him to the bone. "Bring the cloak which I left at Troas," he writes Timothy with a shivering hand, adding poignantly, "Make every effort to come before winter" (2 Tim. 4:13a, 21a).

Paul has been alone before, but intensifying his aloneness is the icy sting of abandonment:

> You are aware of the fact that all who are in Asia turned away from me, among whom are Phyge-lus and Hermogenes. (1:15)

All the Christians from Asia who had stood with him in Rome had fled, leaving him to face by himself the court of senators and counsels and the mad Caesar, Nero. "At my first defense," Paul lamented, "no one supported me, but all deserted me" (4:16a). Certainly some believers, he had hoped, would testify on his behalf; but Nero's bloody purge had begun, and all Paul's friends kept silent for fear of also incurring the emperor's wrath.

Among the deserters were Phygelus and Hermogenes, two names we skim past but which remained fixed in Paul's mind as

---

3. John Pollock, *The Apostle: A Life of Paul* (Wheaton, Ill.: Scripture Press Publications, Victor Books, 1985), p. 304.

piercing reminders of their betrayal. Perhaps the names of certain people who have wronged you haunt your memory. Like Paul, you gave them your life, yet when you were in need, they returned your investment with heartache. If this has happened to you, you can understand Paul's sense of emptiness. He doesn't just feel alone. He feels forsaken, left behind . . . abandoned.

Then he remembers Onesiphorus.

A Friend worth Remembering

> The Lord grant mercy to the house of Onesiphorus
> for he often refreshed me. (1:16a)

In Paul's mind, Onesiphorus was a man who lived up to his name: "one who brings help."[4] The only other time Paul mentions his friend's name is when he instructs Timothy to greet "the household of Onesiphorus" (4:19). Because he sends his greeting to Onesiphorus' family and not to him personally, many scholars conclude that Onesiphorus had died by the time Paul wrote this letter.[5] If so, these verses form Paul's eulogy for a man whose memory he holds dear.

What He Did

Just thinking about Onesiphorus refreshes Paul's heart. The Greek word for *refreshed* in verse 16 of chapter 1 is *anapsuchō*, which means "to cool again." Onesiphorus' presence was like a cool cloth on a burning, wounded spirit. Again and again he came to perform his healing art—"He *often* refreshed me," says Paul.

Ministers of refreshment keep coming back; they don't wait for notes or calls for help. Like intuitive nurses, they know their patients' needs and diligently administer their balm of mercy.

Visiting the famous apostle, however, was no simple matter for Onesiphorus. In the eyes of the state, Paul was a notorious, rabble-rousing criminal. One had to consider carefully the consequences

---

4. *Onesiphorus* is a combination of *oninēmi*, which means "to profit, benefit, help," and the verb *pherō*, which means "to bear or bring." According to G. Abbott-Smith, his name can be translated "bringing advantage." *A Manual Greek Lexicon of the New Testament*, 3d ed. (Edinburgh, Scotland: T. and T. Clark, 1937), p. 318.

5. Support for this conclusion also comes from Paul's prayer for mercy upon "the house of Onesiphorus" (1:16). See William Barclay, *The Letters to Timothy, Titus, and Philemon*, rev. ed., The Daily Study Bible Series (Philadelphia, Pa.: Westminster Press, 1975), p. 156.

of associating with him. But, as Paul proudly writes, Onesiphorus

> was not ashamed of my chains; but when he was in
> Rome, he eagerly searched for me, and found me—
> the Lord grant to him to find mercy from the Lord
> on that day—and you know very well what services
> he rendered at Ephesus. (vv. 16b–18)

To find Paul, Onesiphorus had journeyed by land and sea from Ephesus to Rome. When he arrived at the empire's sprawling capital, though, he was greeted by a tangle of city streets. Somewhere, behind locked doors, was Paul, lost in the Roman judicial system. Commentator P. N. Harrison imagines Onesiphorus' passionate search for his mentor and friend.

> "We seem to catch glimpses of one purposeful face
> in a drifting crowd, and follow with quickening in-
> terest this stranger from the far coasts of the Aegean,
> as he threads the maze of unfamiliar streets, knock-
> ing at many doors, following up every clue, warned
> of the risks he is taking but not to be turned from
> his quest; till in some obscure prison-house a known
> voice greets him, and he discovers Paul chained to
> a Roman soldier. Having once found his way On-
> esiphorus is not content with a single visit, but, true
> to his name, proves unwearied in his ministrations.
> Others have flinched from the menace and igno-
> miny of that chain; but this visitor counts it the
> supreme privilege of his life to share with such a
> criminal the reproach of the Cross."[6]

While many of Paul's friends were hiding behind their doors, brave Onesiphorus sought Paul out. And that search cost him much—perhaps even his life.

How deep is our level of commitment to our friends? Would we have done what Onesiphorus did? Do we have the necessary character qualities? A ministry of refreshment builds upon the blocks of initiative, foresight, unselfishness, and courage. If we stand with someone who is unpopular, winds of disfavor may blow against us as well. Will we be prepared?

If we desire to be like Onesiphorus, we must also ask ourselves:

6. P. N. Harrison, as quoted by Barclay in *The Letters to Timothy, Titus, and Philemon*, pp. 155–56.

Are we afraid of another person's "chains"? Someone who has failed at work may be manacled with the chains of humiliation; a divorced person, the chains of rejection; a prisoner, the chains of disobedience; a falsely accused person, the chains of misunderstanding; a terminally ill person, the chains of awkwardness. Will we be able to look past others' chains?

We don't have to search long to find the prisons in our society. For some people, their hospital room is a prison. A convalescent home can be a prison and so can a CEO's penthouse office. Some can feel imprisoned in their own house or in a relationship. For these people, the walls are closing in. They're losing life's battle, and no one has the courage to stand by them. They need an Onesiphorus to refresh them with hope.

If you decide to pick up the ministry towel that Onesiphorus left at Paul's feet, here is God's promise to you:

> God is not unjust so as to forget your work and the love which you have shown toward His name, in having ministered and in still ministering to the saints. (Heb. 6:10)

Though no one may notice our labors—labors which may seem insignificant in our world—the Lord doesn't forget them. He will reward us someday for the times we sought out the sick at heart to apply a refreshing balm in His name.

Essential Qualities in the Ministry of Refreshment

Becoming a refreshing person may not require a diploma from a prestigious university or years of on-the-job experience. It does, however, necessitate certain character qualifications that anyone can develop. These would include

- *unselfishness:* placing the other person's needs before your own

- *availability:* being willing to give your time

- *sensitivity:* hearing what a person feels and intuitively knowing when you're needed

- *determination:* resolving to help in spite of the obstacles

- *positive attitude:* seeing beyond the present circumstances; being hopeful

- *compassion:* showing tolerance, mercy, and understanding

To those dying of thirst in life's desert, you can be a refreshing cup of encouragement, like Onesiphorus.

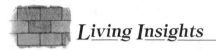 *Living Insights*

In *Kingdoms in Conflict*, Charles Colson and Ellen Santilli Vaughn describe a scene from Aleksandr Solzhenitsyn's novel *The Cancer Ward*—a scene that grimly depicts a world without compassion. In the story,

> a young, cancerous political prisoner named Oleg finds momentary escape from the hospital's horrors in an attractive nurse, Zoya. One day Oleg volunteers to help Zoya with her reports. Reading from patient records, Oleg notices hardly any deaths in the hospital.
>
> "I see they don't allow them to die here," he says. "They manage to discharge them in time."
>
> "What else can they do?" responds Zoya. "Judge for yourself. If it is obvious a patient is beyond help and there is nothing left for him but to live out the few last weeks or months, why should he take up a bed? . . . People who could be cured are kept waiting. . . ."
>
> Days later, one of Oleg's gravely ill friends is told he is being released from the hospital. The man struggles to dress, weakly bids adieu to his comrades, and sets out for the streets. The best he can hope for is an empty bench where he can lie down and wait to die.[7]

The Cancer Ward is far different from the mercy wards of Mother Teresa, where nuns and nurses tenderly dab the sores of lepers and cradle the sick until death. Colson and Vaughn write:

Sometimes [Mother Teresa] is criticized: "Why care

---

7. Charles Colson with Ellen Santilli Vaughn, *Kingdoms in Conflict* (New York, N.Y.: William Morrow; Grand Rapids, Mich.: Zondervan Publishing House, 1987), p. 73.

for those who are doomed anyway?" But she explains, "They are created by God; they deserve to die with dignity."[8]

Why shouldn't we just discard those who have no utilitarian value? Because human worth is intrinsic, breathed into the soul by God. By having compassion on the sick, the dying, the prisoner, and the cast-aside stranger, we are caring for a part of God Himself. Jesus personalized this principle even further:

> "'Truly I say to you, to the extent that you did it to one of these brothers of Mine, even the least of them, you did it to Me.'" (Matt. 25:40)

Take a moment to evaluate your own level of compassion. Do you consider the elderly patients in a convalescent hospital priceless creations of God? Would you be able to love a tattooed prisoner as you would love Jesus? How about an AIDS patient? Or, perhaps closer to home, your recently divorced neighbor?

If you truly desire to begin a ministry of refreshment, you must search your soul with these hard questions. Meditate on Matthew 25:34–40, and ask the Lord to fill you with His compassion.

Living Insights   STUDY TWO

We sometimes forget the power a visit has to encourage those locked in a cell of loneliness. The prisoner, the hospital patient, the grieving—they reach out for human touch, but often, their only companions are the flickering figures on the television screen. How freeing would be the sound of a real voice, the warmth of a genuine smile, and the feeling of spiritual union only you can provide!

In prison, Paul was locked behind the bars of loneliness. His only escape came during dear Onesiphorus' frequent visits. Can you think of someone who desperately needs a visitor?

_____

_____

_____

8. Colson and Vaughn. *Kingdoms in Conflict*, p. 74.

Is it possible to schedule regular times with this person? How would you work out the details?

_____

_____

_____

Can you involve others? What are some ways your friends or family members can take part in your visits?

_____

_____

_____

———◆———

Pure and undefiled religion in the sight of our God and Father is this: to visit orphans and widows in their distress, and to keep oneself unstained by the world. (James 1:27)

Chapter 4

A PLEA FOR INTEGRITY

Daniel 6:1–23

Semper fidelis, "always faithful," is the motto the United States Marine Corps lives and dies by. With this ideal bannered above them, all marines dedicate their lives to honor and country. As they stand at attention in their dress blues, white gloves, and gleaming swords, they proudly display the excellence not only of their ranks but of their commitment as well.

In 1987, however, two marine guards at the U.S. embassy in Moscow threw mud on that brass-buttoned image. In exchange for sexual favors, they allowed Soviet spies to rummage through secret papers, which included military plans, transmission codes, and names of undercover agents. These young marines knew the ethical standard; it had been drilled into them for years. Yet, for a fleeting moment of passion, they eagerly traded it in, along with their own integrity.

Their lapse in character illustrates a broader shift of values in our society. Self-fulfillment has become the highest good, not honor or honesty. According to Charles Colson, one Christian philosopher who saw this day coming was C. S. Lewis.

> He argued in 1943 that mere knowledge of right and wrong is powerless against a person's appetites. Rather, reason must rule the appetites by means of the "spirited element"—that is, loyalty to a transcendent good higher than one's self. Lewis likened reason to the head, the appetite to the stomach, and the spirited element—the essential connecting link— to the chest.
>
> What we are witnessing today is not only the loss of honor or purity among a few individuals, but the loss of the spirited element in society. Lewis summed it up well: "We remove the organ and demand the function. We make men without chests and expect of them virtue and enterprise. We laugh at honor and are shocked to find traitors in our midst."[1]

1. Chuck Colson, *"Semper Fidelis?"* in *Jubilee*, June 1987, pp. 7–8.

As soldiers of the Cross, our loyalty to Christ and His standard should also be nothing less than *semper fidelis*. But how many in our ranks have we seen seduced into society's bed of moral compromise? Our plea is for Christian men and women to treasure and incarnate godly character. To do that, we must begin by defining a word that is at its heart: *integrity*.

Integrity: What It Is and Isn't

The dictionary defines *integrity* as "1: firm adherence to a code of [especially] moral or artistic values: incorruptibility 2: an unimpaired condition: soundness 3: the quality or state of being complete or undivided: completeness."[2] Its Hebrew counterpart, *tom*, has a similar meaning of "completeness." The psalmist uses this word in reference to King David, whom God took from the humble sheepfolds to Israel's throne room:

> So he shepherded them according to the integrity
> of his heart,
> And guided them with his skillful hands. (Ps. 78:72)

No hairline cracks lined David's heart; it was sound, complete. If he made a promise, he kept it. If he began a job, he finished it. With David as a leader, the nation felt secure.

Integrity doesn't imply perfection; David certainly wasn't sinless. However, people with integrity are honest about their failings. They're not hypocritical. As they are in the light, so they are in the dark. They aren't manipulative or self-aggrandizing. And because they have nothing to hide, they don't fear the white light of scrutiny.

Integrity is having the guts to tell the truth, even though it may cost you. It's finding the courage to follow the true path, though others are cutting corners; to endure laughter, embarrassment, or injury for what is right. It's sticking with your beliefs, even if it means being thrown into a lions' den.

Daniel: A Biblical Example

The man of integrity who first faced the lions' den was, of course, Daniel. Let's pick up his story in Daniel 6 and discover some principles that will help us stand strong today.

2. *Merriam-Webster's Collegiate Dictionary*, 10th ed., see "integrity."

Deserved Promotion

Daniel, an exiled Jew, is living in the city of Babylon, which the Medes and Persians have recently conquered. Darius is now king (5:31), and as he reorganizes the government of his realm, he immediately notices the character of Daniel, who is perhaps in his eighties at this time.

> It seemed good to Darius to appoint 120 satraps over the kingdom, that they would be in charge of the whole kingdom, and over them three commissioners (of whom Daniel was one), that these satraps might be accountable to them, and that the king might not suffer loss. Then this Daniel began distinguishing himself among the commissioners and satraps because he possessed an extraordinary spirit, and the king planned to appoint him over the entire kingdom. (6:1–3)

Already one of the three most powerful men in the empire, Daniel is in line to become the next prime minister. Things couldn't have been brighter for this foreigner; yet, paradoxically, Daniel's success couldn't have made his life tougher.

Many of us assume that adversity is the greatest test of our integrity. When money is tight and work is unrewarding and life is a matter of holding on for better days, it seems that finding relief through moral compromise would entice anyone.

A greater test of character, however, is prosperity.[3] Whereas adversity simplifies life to its basics—food, clothing, shelter— prosperity complicates it. When your salary increases, so do your perks, privacy, and temptations. And all the while your enemies are trying to push you back down the ladder. The security you hoped to gain by making it to the top quickly fades. Only the Lord and your integrity will preserve you.

Daniel found this to be true when he encountered prosperity's severest test.

---

3. Scottish essayist Thomas Carlyle wrote: "Adversity is sometimes hard upon a man; but for one man who can stand prosperity, there are a hundred that will stand adversity." As quoted in *Bartlett's Familiar Quotations*, 15th ed., rev. and enl., ed. Emily Morison Beck (Boston, Mass.: Little, Brown and Co., 1980), p. 474.

Undeserved Affliction

Growing jealous of Daniel's favored position, the other commissioners and satraps begin

> trying to find a ground of accusation against Daniel
> in regard to government affairs; but they could find
> no ground of accusation or evidence of corruption,
> inasmuch as he was faithful, and no negligence or
> corruption was to be found in him. (v. 4)

Sifting through Daniel's life, they hope to discover any speck of dirt to use against him. They rifle his files, eavesdrop on his conversations, and tail him twenty-four hours a day. But not one crumb of corruption appears in their sieve. Daniel's life is clean, from his business dealings to his bank accounts to his closed-door meetings. Did Daniel know they were investigating him so closely? Whether or not he noticed his enemies lurking in the shadows, it probably didn't matter to him either way. For he seemed to be following the counsel Eliphaz had given Job years earlier:

> "Is not your fear of God your confidence,
> And the integrity of your ways your hope?" (Job 4:6)

Because he was obedient to God's law, Daniel proved himself blameless under man's law. His enemies' only resort, therefore, is to make obeying God's law a crime.

> Then these men said, "We shall not find any ground
> of accusation against this Daniel unless we find it
> against him with regard to the law of his God."
> (Dan. 6:5)

They convince Darius to sign a thirty-day injunction forbidding prayers to any god or man other than the king. The penalty: a horrible death in the lions' den (vv. 6–9). The king, however, does not realize Daniel's predicament under this new law.

Human Reaction

Upon hearing about the new law, Daniel must choose between following God's law or man's.

> Now when Daniel knew that the document was
> signed, he entered his house (now in his roof chamber he had windows open toward Jerusalem); and he

continued kneeling on his knees three times a day, praying and giving thanks before his God, as he had been doing previously. (v. 10)

By continuing his daily prayers, Daniel risks losing not merely his job, his house, and his prestige—he risks his life. That takes integrity!

The conspirators waste little time informing the king of Daniel's illegal prayers. With delicious pleasure, they remind Darius of his recently signed law, announcing,

"Daniel, who is one of the exiles from Judah, pays no attention to you, O king, or to the injunction which you signed, but keeps making his petition three times a day." (v. 13b)

Can you taste the slanderous venom in their statement? Darius discerns their bitter intentions, but he is powerless to retract his own law to save Daniel (vv. 14–15).

Divine Protection

Then the king gave orders, and Daniel was brought in and cast into the lions' den. (v. 16a)

Is this where a life of integrity and blameless living takes us— to the lions' den? Sometimes. Although we've made the tough decision and done the right thing, we may still feel the hot breath of hardship on our necks. At that point, as King Darius expressed to Daniel, we have just one hope:

"Your God whom you constantly serve will Himself deliver you." (v. 16b)

God did deliver Daniel by sending His angel to clamp shut the mouths of the ravenous lions (v. 22). No harm came to him, "because he had trusted in his God" (v. 23).

You and I: Three Enduring Principles

Long before the founding of the Marine Corps, Daniel was living the motto *semper fidelis*. How we need such examples of integrity! From his story, three enduring principles of this character trait encourage us to follow his lead.

First, *true integrity implies that you do what is right when no one is looking or when everyone else is compromising.* What do you do for a living? Repair cars? Install electrical wiring? Work with numbers? Are you a student? Do you sell clothes? Practice law or medicine? Every occupation requires integrity. Other people may take short-cuts or cheat on the accounts, but a *semper fidelis* Christian maintains a higher standard.

Second, *real integrity stays in place whether the test is adversity or prosperity.* Whether Daniel was next in line to become prime minister or the hungry lions' midnight snack, he maintained his integrity. Are you in the swirl of adversity's need-driven temptations? Or are you ensnarled in prosperity's complications? Remember, real integrity stays in place in good times as well as bad.

Third, *broken integrity means the spiritual leader forfeits the right to lead as he or she once did.* How should we treat leaders who dishonor the name of Christ? There is no doubt that God extends them forgiveness, and so should we. However, the character weakness that contributed to their fall ought to disqualify them from returning to their previously held positions. This is a controversial issue, but it underscores the seriousness of maintaining one's integrity in today's moral climate, particularly for spiritual leaders.[4]

Whether or not you are in a leadership position, if you aspire to keep your integrity in this world, you are a leader. Have courage. No matter which way the political and social winds blow, stay faithful.

Always faithful. *Semper fidelis.*

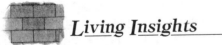 ## Living Insights

In *Strengthening Your Grip,* Charles Swindoll tells the following story about integrity and a box of fried chicken.

> Some time ago, I heard about a fellow in Long Beach who went into a fried chicken franchise to get some chicken for himself and the young lady with him. She waited in the car while he went in to pick up the chicken. Inadvertently, the manager

---

4. For a complete discussion of Insight for Living's perspective concerning the restoration of fallen leaders, please see the study guide *Christ at the Crossroads,* written by Lee Hough, from the Bible-teaching ministry of Charles R. Swindoll (Anaheim, Calif.: Insight for Living, 1991), pp. 128–31.

of the store handed the guy the box in which he had placed the financial proceeds of the day instead of the box of chicken. You see, he was going to make a deposit and had camouflaged it by putting the money in a fried chicken box.

The fellow took his box, went back to the car, and the two of them drove away. When they got to the park and opened the box, they discovered they had a box full of money. Now that's a very vulnerable moment for the average individual. He realized there must have been a mistake, so he got back in his car and returned to the place and gave the money back to the manager. Well, the manager was elated! He was so pleased that he told the young man, "Stick around, I want to call the newspaper and have them take your picture. You're the most honest guy in town."

"Oh, no, don't do that!" said the fellow.

"Why not?" asked the manager.

"Well," he said, "you see, I'm married, and the woman I'm with is not my wife!"[5]

This story illustrates a vital point about integrity: Appearances can be deceiving! On the surface of our lives, we may show signs of integrity. We return money that's not ours. We give ourselves to our family and church. But if someone were to write a story about our lives, would we really want them to print *everything?*

Many Christians do not harbor secrets. They are the Daniels in whom "no ground of accusation or evidence of corruption" can be found (Dan. 6:4). You may be one of them, and we encourage you to guard your integrity—it's priceless.

Many other Christians, though, are nurturing hidden vices that undermine their integrity and decay their consciences. Sadly, the majority of these believers never seek help . . . until they're caught.

According to Solomon's wise counsel,

> He who conceals his transgressions will not prosper,
> But he who confesses and forsakes them will find
>   compassion. (Prov. 28:13)

5. Charles R. Swindoll, *Strengthening Your Grip* (Dallas, Tex.: Word Publishing, 1982), pp. 99–100.

Today, if you're sheltering secret sin, tell someone you can trust who can help you restore your integrity. God's compassion may surprise you.

Living Insights STUDY TWO

Like glass, vows shatter when we break them, cutting those nearby. The razorlike shards often lodge beneath the skin, becoming painful reminders of our tossed-aside promises.

"I don't love you anymore—I don't think I ever did."

"The business deal is off."

"I don't believe in God anymore. I'm leaving the church."

Have you been the victim of a broken vow? If so, you can probably recall the exact words said, because you still have the scars. Sometimes we think we can back out of our commitments without harming anyone. We say, "She'll get over it," or, "He'll find someone new." But breaking a vow is a serious matter; some people never recover.

Because others depend on you, we plead with you to keep your promises and maintain your integrity. Take a few moments to write down the vows you have made. Use this time to recommit yourself to staying faithful, no matter what. And pray for the Lord's courage. Thankfully, He has never broken His vows. And He never will.

1. _____

   _____

2. _____

   _____

3. _____

   _____

4. _____

   _____

Chapter 5

REINSTATEMENT OF A RUNAWAY

Philemon

A flower unfurls its petals to greet the rising sun. Young forest animals shed their newborn fuzz to reveal a coat of adult fur. The soft earth swells with bursting life as the seed puts forth its first shoots.

New beginnings. Nature thrives on them. Our lives depend on them.

Spiritually, we experience a new beginning when we believe in Christ. At that moment, darkness retreats before the stretching rays of His sun and new life erupts in our souls. The apostle Paul witnessed this spiritual dawn in the life of a runaway slave named Onesimus. Shrouded in darkness, Onesimus first came to him fearful and guilt-ridden. Then he received Christ's seed, and a strong, new character blossomed in his life.

Let's witness this transformation as recounted by Paul himself in a letter to Onesimus' owner, Philemon. It's a letter sown with hope for a runaway slave who must develop the courage to face his past.

Background

As we unfold Paul's letter to Philemon, it will be helpful to understand the context of this personal correspondence. Paul, who had been arrested in Jerusalem following his third missionary journey, had endured a number of trials over a two-year period and was eventually transported to Rome. While awaiting a hearing before Caesar, he was under house arrest in his own rented quarters but was able to present the gospel to his guards and all who came to visit him (see Acts 28:16–31). One of his visitors was a slave named Onesimus.

At that time in the Roman Empire, nearly sixty million slaves labored in the fields, shops, and homes of their owners. Their lot in

---

This chapter is an adaptation of "A Postcard to Philemon," from the study guide *New Testament Postcards*, written by Ken Gire, from the Bible-teaching ministry of Charles R. Swindoll (Fullerton, Calif.: Insight for Living, 1986), pp. 1–7.

life was not an easy one, as commentator William Barclay explains.

> A slave was not a person; he was a living tool. A master had absolute power over his slaves. "He can box their ears or condemn them to hard labour—making them, for instance, work in chains upon his lands in the country, or in a sort of prison-factory. Or, he may punish them with blows of the rod, the lash or the knot."[1]

And for slaves who ran away from their masters, the punishment was even more severe.

> If a slave ran away, at best he would be branded with a red-hot iron on the forehead, with the letter F—standing for *fugitivus*, *runaway*—and at the worst he would be crucified.[2]

As a fugitive slave, Onesimus was already in serious trouble, but to make matters worse, he apparently had stolen something from Philemon to finance his flight (see Philem. 18). So when the young thief embarked on his hazardous twelve-hundred-mile journey from Colossae to Rome, he left knowing one thing for certain: he could never return.

Then he met Paul.

Befriending this runaway rebel, the Apostle introduced him to the Savior, in whom "there is neither slave nor free man" (Gal. 3:28b). Onesimus believed in Christ and was immediately transformed.

Paul, however, now faces a dilemma. To keep Onesimus would be beneficial, yet the slave's rightful place is with his master, Paul's friend Philemon. The Apostle decides Onesimus must do the courageous and ethical thing: return home. In a letter that Onesimus himself will deliver to his disgruntled master, Paul defends the repentant thief.

---

1. William Barclay, *The Letters to Timothy, Titus, and Philemon*, rev. ed., The Daily Study Bible Series (Philadelphia, Pa.: Westminster Press, 1975), p. 270. By the first century, a slave's lot had improved. Although still seen as commodities, slaves were often educated, trained in a trade, turned into useful members of society, and sometimes even freed. However, impatient Onesimus could wait for none of those privileges.

2. Barclay, *Letters to Timothy, Titus, and Philemon*, p. 270.

Introduction

Paul's short, gracious note begins humbly and affectionately.

> Paul, a prisoner of Christ Jesus, and Timothy our
> brother, to Philemon our beloved brother and fellow
> worker, and to Apphia our sister, and to Archippus
> our fellow soldier, and to the church in your house:
> Grace to you and peace from God our Father and
> the Lord Jesus Christ. (Philem. 1–3)

The Apostle quietly reveals his unshakable faith by referring to himself as a prisoner of Jesus Christ, seeing beyond the Roman guard to God's overarching purpose.[3] Then we get our first glimpse of Philemon, whom Paul calls "our beloved brother," because, like Onesimus, he was one of his converts (v. 19). Philemon's home was probably used for church meetings; and apparently Apphia, who was possibly his wife, and Archippus, possibly his son, both assisted in the ministry. In verse 3, Paul bids Philemon "grace" and "peace." Both words strengthen Paul's plea, because as he appeals to the Father and the Son to show grace and peace to Philemon, so his appeal to Philemon is based on the grace and peace he should show Onesimus.[4]

Commendation

In the next verses, Paul commends Philemon, showing him why he considers him a beloved brother and fellow worker. Here the letter focuses on Philemon, emphasizing Paul's key phrase: "I thank my God."

> I thank my God always, making mention of you
> in my prayers, because I hear of your love of the faith
> which you have toward the Lord Jesus and toward
> all the saints; and I pray that the fellowship of your
> faith may become effective through the knowledge
> of every good thing which is in you for Christ's sake.
> For I have come to have much joy and comfort in
> your love, because the hearts of the saints have been

---

3. Paul also wrote his epistles to the Ephesians, Philippians, and Colossians—commonly called the prison epistles—during this first imprisonment in Rome.

4. Applying this further, as much as we long for peace in our lives and in our world, there can be no peace without first receiving God's grace in our hearts. Grace always precedes peace.

refreshed through you, brother. (vv. 4–7)

Philemon's home was an oasis of refreshment to the believers who worshiped there, and the cool breezes of his "love" reached twelve hundred miles across the barren empire to fill Paul with "comfort" and "joy."

Intercession

Having encouraged Philemon, Paul changes the focus in verses 8–16 to Onesimus, the runaway. His key phrase appears in verse 10: "I appeal to you." He does not pull rank on Philemon by listing his credentials as an apostle; rather, he appeals to him on the basis of love.

> Therefore, though I have enough confidence in Christ to order you to do that which is proper, yet for love's sake I rather appeal to you—since I am such a person as Paul, the aged, and now also a prisoner of Christ Jesus—I appeal to you for my child Onesimus, whom I have begotten in my imprisonment. (vv. 8–10)

Onesimus—a name that grates over Philemon's tongue and leaves the bitter aftertaste of disloyalty and desertion. Paul waits until now to mention his name, and he wisely sweetens the word with the phrase "my child, whom I have begotten in my imprisonment." No man ever asked for fewer favors than did Paul. But in this letter he asks a favor, not so much for himself as for Onesimus, who had taken a wrong turn in his life. Now, Paul was helping him find the way back.

In verse 11, the Apostle reveals to Philemon the change that has taken place in Onesimus' life as a result of his new birth in Christ:

> [He] formerly was useless to you, but now is useful both to you and to me.

The one picture of Onesimus that remained with Philemon was of the *useless* Onesimus of the past—a runaway and a thief (vv. 15, 18). A more recent photo, however, which Paul provides in the following verses, shows a radically changed Onesimus.

> I have sent him back to you in person, that is, sending my very heart, whom I wished to keep with me,

so that on your behalf he might minister to me in my imprisonment for the gospel; but without your consent I did not want to do anything, so that your goodness would not be, in effect, as it were by compulsion but of your own free will. For perhaps he was for this reason parted from you for a while, that you should have him back forever, no longer as a slave, but more than a slave, a beloved brother, especially to me, but how much more to you, both in the flesh and in the Lord. (vv. 12–16)

The eight-by-ten Paul is sending to Philemon is of the *useful* Onesimus—a minister and a beloved brother (vv. 13, 16). What a transformation! It is on the basis of this picture that Paul pleads with Philemon to forgive Onesimus and accept him again into his home.

Obligation

At verse 17, the focus shifts again and Paul becomes the main character. The key phrase is "I will repay" (v. 19a), for the Apostle now takes on the role of Onesimus' advocate.

According to a clause in Roman law known as *advocacy*, runaway slaves could return to their masters and be protected if they first went to the master's friend and secured support for their cause. The friend then became an advocate, or mediator, who appealed to the slave's owner for grace and understanding. There were even some instances where the slave owner not only accepted the slave back but went as far as to adopt the slave. Apparently, this clause is what verses 15–16 refer to. Paul hopes Philemon will accept Onesimus with the open arms of a brother, not only in the spiritual sense—"in the Lord"—but in the physical sense as well—"in the flesh" (v. 16).

Paul's appeal grows even stronger in verse 17, where he puts his request in the framework of his and Philemon's relationship.

> If then you regard me a partner, accept him as you would me.

And finally, pulling out all the stops, he offers his own wallet on Onesimus' behalf:

> But if he has wronged you in any way or owes you anything, charge that to my account; I, Paul, am

writing this with my own hand, I will repay it (not to mention to you that you owe to me even your own self as well). Yes, brother, let me benefit from you in the Lord; refresh my heart in Christ. (vv. 18–20)

Though the English doesn't reveal it, Paul uses a subtle play on words in verse 20. *Benefit* is the root word of Onesimus' name. Essentially, Paul is saying, "You have benefited from me spiritually, and now I am also sending Onesimus to you, my friend, all debts paid. So let me, in return, receive from you a touch of 'onesimus' through your willingness to forgive him."

Then, in verses 21–24, Paul concludes his note with confidence that Philemon will do the right thing, and he sends his greetings to other believers in Colossae. As a postscript, he lovingly leaves Philemon with this prayer: "The grace of the Lord Jesus Christ be with your spirit" (v. 25).

Conclusion

For a moment, put yourself in Philemon's sandals. Onesimus has wronged you, broken your trust, and stolen from you. "Useless Onesimus" is his name as far as you're concerned. Now he has returned. Would you give him a second chance?

Now, in a broader sense, put yourself in God's place. All of humankind has wronged you, broken your trust, and stolen from you. Would you have the love to give the world a second chance? Through Jesus Christ, God did just that. In many ways, the ancient letter to Philemon has a present-day postmark, with our names on the forwarding address.

Practical Truths

Every Christian was once a fugitive. Every Christian was once enslaved to sin, a runaway from birth. Like sheep, we had all gone our own way rather than God's (Isa. 53:6).

Our guilt was heavy and the penalty severe. Like Onesimus, we lived in fear of being punished for our crimes against God. Guilt hounded our conscience no matter how far from home we ran. Without Christ, we would have died in our sins, facing the eternal emptiness and torment of hell.

Grace allowed the right of appeal. Alone in our death-row cell, we waited for our sentence to be carried out. But pleading our case was our advocate, Jesus Christ, who stood before His Father, the

Judge, and mediated on our behalf (see 1 Tim. 2:5).

Christ said, "Charge that to My account!" Hanging in agony on the cross, He paid the debt we owe the Father for our sins (see Col. 2:13–14).

As a result, our Master—our original Owner—accepted us back. Because of Christ's death and resurrection, we have been accepted back by the Father and adopted as His children (Gal. 4:5).

Historical Truths

We can't leave our study of this compelling letter without wondering what happened to Onesimus. Thumbing through the New Testament mail, we might expect to find a quick postcard from Philemon with his reply to Paul, but it is nowhere to be found. However, a church father named Ignatius, writing fifty years later in a letter to the Ephesians, addressed their wonderful minister, their bishop, named Onesimus. In this letter, according to commentator William Barclay,

> Ignatius makes exactly the same pun as Paul made—
> he is Onesimus by name and Onesimus by nature,
> the profitable one to Christ. It may well be that the
> runaway slave had become with the passing years
> the great bishop of Ephesus.[5]

If that is true, Bishop Onesimus of Ephesus may have played a large role in insisting that this slip of a letter be included in the New Testament canon. We can imagine the honorable Onesimus announcing: "I want the world to know my story—how a useless runaway slave became useful through the transforming power of the Cross."

If Jesus Christ can make "useless" slaves like Onesimus useful again, what new beginnings can He bring about in your life? With Him, anything can happen.

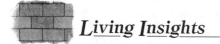 *Living Insights* STUDY ONE

Can you identify with Onesimus? Perhaps you feel useless—too far gone to be of benefit to the Lord or anyone else. Like a runaway slave, you may wander through life doing whatever you please, but

---

5. Barclay, *Letters to Timothy, Titus, and Philemon*, p. 275.

your soul is chained to past failures or feelings of worthlessness. You desperately want to break free. But how?

Onesimus did not really breathe freedom's pure air until he gave his life to Christ. At that moment, in Paul's words, he became "a new creature; the old things passed away; behold, new things have come" (2 Cor. 5:17b).

The world may tell you that you are too far gone. Even Christians may shake their heads and add you to their list of hopeless cases. But as long as there is breath in your lungs, you have the potential of being transformed into someone worthy and useful.

Won't you surrender your life to Christ right now? If you don't have the strength to face your past, let His courage be your courage. Let His confidence be your confidence.

One last thing: Onesimus leaned on his brother Paul to help build his sense of value and character. Ask the Lord to help you find a partner who can encourage you to be a useful servant of Christ.

Living Insights

Paul's little letter to Philemon gives us a hope-filled picture of Onesimus; but if we look at it again from another angle, we'll also find a portrait of Paul's compassion. Before his conversion, the cold-hearted Pharisee Saul had all the compassion of a Nazi. But when Christ's mercy blinded him, he opened his eyes and saw a new world before him in which all people had value, including thieving runaway slaves.

How is your CQ—Compassion Quotient? Are there certain people or groups of people you have difficulty accepting?

_____

_____

Paul's secret for keeping compassion's fires glowing was to fuel his mind with humility and gratitude. Read 1 Timothy 1:12–17 and feel the warmth of these two traits together.

Read this passage again, only this time imagine you had written these words instead of Paul. Let each "I" and "me" in the verses refer to yourself.

What new insights do you gain regarding God's compassion toward you?

_____

_____

_____

Does being embraced by God's compassion help you see others in a more compassionate light? In what ways?

_____

_____

_____

While Christians with high IQs may impress the world with their intellects, those with high CQs win the world with their love. Christ would have it that way.

Chapter 6

COPING WITH THE "SLOUGH OF DESPOND"

1 Kings 19

John Bunyan's classic allegory of the Christian life, *The Pilgrim's Progress*, follows the hero, Christian, on his treacherous journey from the City of Destruction to his heavenly destination, the Celestial City. Along the way, Christian and a companion approach

> a very miry slough, that was in the midst of the plain; and they being heedless, did both fall suddenly into the bog. The name of the slough was Despond. Here, therefore, they wallowed for a time, being grievously bedaubed with dirt; and Christian, because of the burden that was on his back, began to sink in the mire.[1]

His traveling companion manages to get out, but rather than giving Christian a hand up, he turns away from the path of life and flees home. Christian, then, is left struggling alone in the boggy, muddy hole until a man named Help—the Holy Spirit—kindly pulls him free from despondency's pit and sets him on solid ground.

Christian asks Help why this dangerous plot of land has not been "mended, that poor travellers might go" on heaven's journey "with more security?" And Help tellingly replies: "This miry slough is such a place as cannot be mended."[2]

How true this is in real life! No matter how hard we try or how spiritually mature we are, miry sloughs are inevitable. Not because we have failed somehow, but because no one is immune to despondency; it is "such a place as cannot be mended"—only traveled through. And that is true even for those with great character.

Consider Moses, God's chosen emancipator and leader of Israel's thousands—even he lost hope and asked God to kill him (Num. 11). Paul, too, the great apostle of grace, confessed that he "despaired even of life" while ministering in Asia (2 Cor. 1:8). And finally, the man we will visit in this chapter, the rugged prophet Elijah,

---

1. John Bunyan, *The Pilgrim's Progress* (1688; reprint, Old Tappan, N.J.: Fleming H. Revell Co., Spire Books, n.d.), p. 7.

2. Bunyan, *The Pilgrim's Progress*, p. 8.

who after triumphing over the prophets of Baal on Mount Carmel (1 Kings 18), ran away and curled up under a juniper tree, waiting to die.

How can this happen to such exemplary saints of God? How does this happen to you and to me? Let's track Elijah's descent into despondency and see what lessons God has for us there.

Setting the Scene

Several personalities play key roles in Elijah's journey into the "slough" and out: King Ahab, Queen Jezebel, Elijah, and the Lord.

Ahab. Frightened and worried after the events on Mount Carmel, Ahab rushes home to his wife, Jezebel, and breathlessly tattles on Elijah for embarrassing him and destroying all of his false prophets (19:1).

Jezebel. Quickly taking matters into her own domineering hands, Jezebel defends her weak husband with a vengeance—and staunchly remains in rebellion against the true God. In a matter of minutes, she dispatches a threatening edict to the mighty prophet Elijah:

> "So may the gods do to me and even more, if I do
> not make your life as the life of one of [the dead
> prophets] by tomorrow about this time." (v. 2)

Elijah. And what is Elijah's response? He had just faced an entire nation who opposed him; he had single-handedly executed the 450 prophets of Baal (18:22, 40); and when he had prayed for rain on a cloudless day, torrents flooded the earth. He had even outrun Ahab and his chariot back to Jezreel (vv. 45–46). You would think he'd be rejoicing on a mountain of unshakable faith. But when he heard Jezebel's threat,

> he was afraid and arose and ran for his life and came
> to Beersheba, which belongs to Judah, and left his
> servant there. (19:3)

Beersheba was about a hundred miles south of Jezreel, but that still wasn't far enough away from wicked Jezebel. So Elijah went even farther into the wilderness; and there he sat, all alone, under a juniper tree. And he prayed to die (v. 4).

Analysis of Despondency

As we look at this poor soul longing for death's relief, we ache with him because we have visited that same wilderness and yearned for heaven's release. So, for a few moments, let's examine five factors that led to his despondency—factors that sometimes surface in our lives as well.

Elijah Didn't Think Clearly or Realistically

When threatened by Jezebel, Elijah didn't consider the source—a person who was God's enemy, an idol worshiper, and one who had no authority over God's elect. Elijah also did not question the threat itself, which could have been a bluff. Most important, though, Elijah neglected to call upon the Lord. Like us in stressful situations, he forgot to stop and pray. Had he fallen on his knees before hightailing it south, he might have recaptured his sense of perspective.

Elijah Separated Himself from Strengthening Relationships

Although Elijah had kept his servant with him until Beersheba, he went into the wilderness alone. Most beds underneath juniper trees are single beds, and most discouraged people are alone more than they should be. Despondency feeds on loneliness, for we are most susceptible to its damaging effects when we are isolated from the strength friendships can bring (see Eccles. 4:9–12).

Elijah Was Caught in the Aftermath of a Victory

After a great victory, we are often vulnerable to times of despair. Elijah was no exception. Everything in his life had been building up to the confrontation on Mount Carmel; now that it was over, what was he supposed to do?

Elijah Was Physically and Emotionally Spent

During the last few years, Elijah's ministry had been full-speed ahead. And in the last few days, he had been riding the red-eye without any rest. When his adrenaline dried up, though, he was left physically and emotionally burned out. For those of us who work harder than we should and live by the rule that enough is never enough, we would do well to remember the old Greek motto: You will break the bow if you keep it always bent.

Elijah Submitted to the Beast, Self-Pity

Look at his words in 1 Kings 19:4:

> "It is enough; now, O Lord, take my life, for I am not better than my fathers."

47

Who said he had to be better than his fathers? Perfection was *his* standard, not God's standard. So when he came up short, he felt sorry for himself.

At this point, some of us might be tempted to take Elijah by the shoulders and lovingly shake some sense into him. But the Lord had a different method.

Response of the Lord

As Help did with Christian, the Lord gently picked Elijah up and set him on his feet again. Let's learn from God's compassionate response.

He Allowed Him Rest and Refreshment

Physical needs are real needs, and meeting these was God's first course of action.

> [Elijah] lay down and slept under a juniper tree; and behold, there was an angel touching him, and he said to him, "Arise, eat." Then he looked and behold, there was at his head a bread cake baked on hot stones, and a jar of water. So he ate and drank and lay down again. The angel of the Lord came again a second time and touched him and said, "Arise, eat, because the journey is too great for you." So he arose and ate and drank, and went in the strength of that food forty days and forty nights to Horeb, the mountain of God. (vv. 5–8)

"You need nourishment, Elijah, you need rest," the Lord says. But notice what He doesn't say. He doesn't interrupt with a sermon, nor does He question Elijah's feelings. He doesn't compare him with those less fortunate, nor does He heap shame on him. God just lets him be human, and He takes care of those human needs.

For some of us "super-Christians," this is essential to grasp. One author comments:

> We have become so compulsively utilitarian that we can scarcely hear, see, or feel the world about us without having to attach a purpose to it. If we can't, at least at times, do something totally purposeless, perhaps it is because we do not really believe in the sovereignty of God. Possibly we're taking ourselves

too seriously, placing too much importance on our-selves and the work we are doing. Yes, God works through people, but our work isn't the only reason God created us. We can trust God to continue his ultimate purposes for a little while even without our sweat.[3]

He Communicated with Elijah Tenderly and Wisely

Look again at verse 7, where the angel of the Lord comes to Elijah a second time. Gently touching him, He says, "Arise, eat, because the journey is too great for you." That's a sweet response, a tender recognition of Elijah's condition. And so, strengthened and rested, Elijah journeys on to Mount Horeb,[4] where the Lord speaks to him again.

> He came there to a cave, and lodged there; and be-hold, the word of the Lord came to him, and He said to him, "What are you doing here, Elijah?" (v. 9)

Elijah laments that he is all alone, the only prophet of the Lord still alive (v. 10); but instead of contradicting him, God uses a different strategy.[5]

> So He said, "Go forth, and stand on the mountain before the Lord." And behold, the Lord was passing by! And a great and strong wind was rending the mountains and breaking in pieces the rocks before the Lord; but the Lord was not in the wind. And after the wind an earthquake, but the Lord was not in the earthquake. And after the earthquake a fire, but the Lord was not in the fire; and after the fire a sound of a gentle blowing. And when Elijah heard it, he wrapped his face in his mantle and went out and stood in the entrance of the cave. And behold, a voice came to him and said, "What are you doing here, Elijah?" (vv. 11–13)

---

3. Tim Hansel, *When I Relax I Feel Guilty* (Elgin, Ill.: David C. Cook Publishing Co., 1979), p. 60.

4. Mount Horeb is also known as Mount Sinai and has always been a significant meeting place for God and His people (see Exod. 3; 19; 20).

5. In 1 Kings 18:13, we learn that in actuality Elijah knew of one hundred prophets of the Lord who were hidden from Jezebel by Obadiah, Ahab's believing servant.

Discouraged people are fragile people, not rugged. They're like delicate pieces of fine china, needing to be handled gently. As the Lord models for us here, we don't have to raise our voices to get the attention of a despondent friend; we can come in the gentleness of a soft breeze.

Elijah, however, is still wrestling with his feelings. Again he repeats his melancholy refrain, "I alone am left; and they seek my life, to take it away" (v. 14b). Graciously, mercifully, God gives His prophet a glimpse of the future—a glimpse that reassures him of his place and purpose in God's plan (vv. 15–17). Then He patiently corrects him about his aloneness, revealing that He has seven thousand in Israel who have resisted the corruption of Baal (v. 18).

He Gave Him a Close, Personal Friend

Verse 19 tells us that Elijah "departed from there and found Elisha," a kindred spirit who would stay with Elijah the rest of his life. How welcome he was to Elijah's heart.

> And Elijah passed over to him and threw his mantle on him. . . . Then [Elisha] arose and followed Elijah and ministered to him. (vv. 19b, 21b)

With his physical needs met, his broken perspective gently set, and someone to help shoulder the load of ministry, Elijah was now out of the slough and back on solid ground.

Final Thought

Many of us readily recognize our need for rest and for time spent in quietness with God. But too often, we try to take on the world alone rather than acknowledge our need for help. We underestimate the power of one life on another. However, if Elijah needed an Elisha; Moses needed an Aaron; and Paul needed a Barnabas, a Silas, a Timothy, and a Luke; then it's clear that we need others too.

Sloughs of despond that "cannot be mended" are certain to be strewn throughout our lives. But who knows how much their depth and our length of time in them can be lessened by a godly companion?

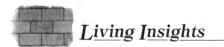 *Living Insights* STUDY ONE

The first and best way to cope with a slough of despond is not to fall into one in the first place! To help us avoid the slough's slippery banks, let's apply Elijah's case to our own lives.

- The first step that mired Elijah was a lack of clear, realistic thinking. In short, he lost his perspective. All too often, when difficult circumstances barge onto our path, they become all we see. What sort of thoughts stomp through your mind when you encounter difficulties? Don't be shy if they seem ridiculous or absurd; only when you can see how exaggerated they really are can you cut them down to size.

_____

_____

_____

- Next, Elijah separated himself from strengthening relationships. With the weight of the universe planted squarely on our shoulders, we, too, often find it hard to remember the many people who care about us. What godly, dependable people can you turn to in times of trouble?

_____

_____

- If your list is shorter than you would like, or if no one comes to mind, this may be an area that needs your attention. Keeping in mind that these types of relationships don't come quickly or casually, brainstorm some ways you can enlarge your base of support.

_____

_____

_____

- Third, Elijah was caught in the aftermath of a great victory. In what ways can you refresh yourself after a demanding achievement?

_____

_____

_____

- Fourth, Elijah was physically exhausted and emotionally spent. Right now, how do you rate your physical condition? Are you emotionally drained?

_____

If someone you love were in your condition, what would you recommend?

_____

_____

Now, do that for yourself.

- The last step that drove Elijah neck deep into the bog was submitting to self-pity. One excellent way to keep your head above water is to maintain your sense of humor. This doesn't mean making a joke of your situation—there was nothing funny in Jezebel's murderous threat. Rather, it's seeing the absurdity of self-pity's overdramatics: "I alone am left," Elijah wailed. What favorite scenario does self-pity like to reenact on the stage of your heart? As you set the scene, let your sense of humor help you ring down the curtain on self-pity's power.

_____

_____

_____

 Living Insights   STUDY TWO

Arthur Gordon, in his book *A Touch of Wonder,* relates a story he was told that beautifully describes the impact one life can have on another. The man Gordon spoke with had been stricken with polio at age three, and his parents, probably Depression-poor and overwhelmed, had abandoned him at a New York City hospital. Taken in by a foster family, he was sent to stay with their relatives in Georgia when he was six, in hopes that the warmer climate would improve his condition. What improved his condition, though, was Maum Jean, an elderly, African-American woman who took that "frail, lost, lonely little boy" into her heart.[6] For six years, she daily

6. Arthur Gordon, *A Touch of Wonder* (Old Tappan, N.J.: Fleming H. Revell Co., 1974), p. 122.

massaged his weak legs; administered her own hydrotherapy in a nearby creek; and encouraged him spiritually with her stories, songs, and prayers.

"Night after night Maum Jean continued the massaging and praying. Then one morning, when I was about twelve, she told me she had a surprise for me.

"She led me out into the yard and placed me with my back against an oak tree; I can feel the rough bark of it to this day. She took away my crutches and braces. She moved back a dozen paces and told me that the Lord had spoken to her in a dream. He had said that the time had come for me to walk. 'So now,' said Maum Jean, 'I want you to walk over here to me.'

"My instant reaction was fear. I knew I couldn't walk unaided; I had tried. I shrank back against the solid support of the tree. Maum Jean continued to urge me.

"I burst into tears. I begged. I pleaded. Her voice rose suddenly, no longer gentle and coaxing but full of power and command. 'You can walk, boy! The Lord has spoken! Now walk over here.'

"She knelt down and held out her arms. And somehow, impelled by something stronger than fear, I took a faltering step, and another, and another, until I reached Maum Jean and fell into her arms, both of us weeping.

"It was two more years before I could walk normally, but I never used the crutches again. . . .

". . . All that happened a long time ago. I live in another town, now. But I still think of Maum Jean often, and the main thing she taught me: that nothing is a barrier when love is strong enough. Not age. Not race. Not anything."[7]

Is God calling you to be a Maum Jean in a frail, young life? Or an Elisha in the life of a despondent prophet? Heed His call, and never underestimate the power of your touch on another.

7. Gordon, *A Touch of Wonder*, pp. 123–25.

Chapter 7

BEING A BALANCED WOMAN OF GOD

Selected Scriptures

In their book *Rocking the Roles: Building a Win-Win Marriage*, Robert Lewis and William Hendricks paint a vivid portrait of today's overextended woman:

> For a while, women were told they could "do it all." "Super Moms" and "Super Women," they were called. But it turned out to be a "Super Myth." One woman [said], "I'm spread so thin right now, I don't know if there's anything left to devote to anything else. I'm an overworked professional, an overtired mother, a part-time wife, and a fair-weather friend!" The promise of having it all has led many women to a great deal of exhaustion, guilt, and heartache.[1]

We like to poke fun at television's apron-clad woman of the 1950s, with her tidy home, Howdy Doody kids, and charming husband. But isn't the modern superwoman ideal just as unrealistic? For many women, stretching themselves between home and career has been like putting one foot on the dock and one foot in the boat. It's not easy to stay balanced!

Several Observations

In general, we can observe six ways women respond to today's unrealistic expectations.

1. Some women are angry about the dirty deal they've gotten. Harassed on the job and unfairly treated just because they are women, they build walls of bitterness against men . . . and God.

2. Other women lack discernment and clear thinking, listening more to talk shows than to God's Word.

1. Robert Lewis and William Hendricks, *Rocking the Roles: Building a Win-Win Marriage* (Colorado Springs, Colo.: NavPress, 1991), p. 94.

3. Still others have scorned their femininity altogether and have become masculine militants.

4. Some, out of fear, have faded into passivity, becoming living doormats.

5. Perhaps most women simply are confused about their roles. They attend seminars, read books, and listen to tapes, hoping to see some light through the fog.

6. And finally, a few women—whether homemakers or career women, single or married—feel comfortable with their roles and may even wonder what all the fuss is about.

Do you see yourself or someone you know in the preceding descriptions? Bring your frustrations and questions to God's Word, and let's allow it to tell us what women need in order to establish balance in their lives. We'll begin by highlighting two unbiblical extremes women should avoid.

Two Extremes—Neither Very Attractive

As we've stated, some women react to the confusion of roles by being overly aggressive, dominant, or militant. Unwilling to be led, especially by a man, they become defensive, angry, and sometimes even paranoid that men are trying to hurt them or deny their rights. Sadly, this behavior drives people away, causing further unhappiness and loneliness. Such can be the results of this secular mentality.

The other extreme is a blind, traditional mentality. These women choose an inordinately passive role, which they believe is biblical. Living behind a veil of fear, they lack the confidence to state their opinions or make independent decisions. To them, submission means bowing to the whims of their husbands while sacrificing their own dignity. If their husbands die or divorce them, or their children leave the nest, they're not prepared to face the world on their own. Tragically, by lowering themselves to the level of slaves, they truly think they are obeying God's will. Like the previous extreme, though, this role flows from contaminated sources of information.

What Has Caused Such Extremism?

We can track these extremes to four poisoned springs. First, we discover *a misunderstanding and misapplication of "submission."*

Submitting ourselves to one another should raise our self-esteem, not lower it. However, some pastors, so-called authorities, husbands, and even wives have taught a degrading type of submissiveness God never intended.

Second, we find *a failure on the part of men to do three things: think clearly, lead fairly, and release unselfishly.* Scripture's model for men is Jesus, who treated women with dignity whether they were pure in heart or prostitutes. Warming them with His compassion, He released women to serve God according to their abilities. If men treated women as the Bible instructs, much of the extremism among women would vanish.

A third source of extremism is *a strong action from the world to "liberate" all women.* By perpetuating the superwoman myth, the media machine hammers into women its way of thinking. "Free the oppressed homemaker!" is the cry. Suddenly, women who love working in their homes are made to feel enslaved and inferior.

Finally, *an equally strong resistance on the part of the church to keep any independence from happening.* Sometimes we view the role of women through the stained-glass spectacles of church tradition rather than the clear lens of God's Word. We must be careful not to take a stand against a role that may be new to us simply because "we've never done it that way before."

Balance—A Scriptural Analysis

Unlike these polluted sources of information, one source issues pure, refreshing truth: God's Word. Looking to a few women in the New Testament as models, let's dip our hands into that spring and draw out some traits that characterize the balanced woman of God.

Concerning Scripture

The first woman we'll meet is Timothy's mother, Eunice. Paul got acquainted with her while visiting Lystra during his second missionary journey.

> And a certain disciple was there, named Timothy,
> the son of a Jewish woman who was a believer, but
> his father was a Greek. (Acts 16:1b)

That little word *but* subtly reveals a contrast between Eunice and her husband. She was a Jewish believer, *but* he was a Greek un-believer. Ethnically, culturally, and spiritually, they were opposites.

Any Christian woman in an interfaith marriage can understand the challenges Eunice faced, particularly in her efforts to raise godly children. Under her wing, though, Timothy believed in Christ and "was well spoken of by the brethren who were in Lystra and Iconium" (v. 2).

How did Eunice manage this? In Paul's second letter to Timothy, we get a glimpse of one aspect of her influence.

> I am mindful of the sincere faith within you, which first dwelt in your grandmother Lois and your mother Eunice, and I am sure that it is in you as well. (2 Tim. 1:5)

Both she and her mother passed their faith on to Timothy. According to Paul,

> from childhood you have known the sacred writings which are able to give you the wisdom that leads to salvation through faith which is in Christ Jesus. (2 Tim. 3:15)

Paul traced Timothy's strong faith directly to the biblical wisdom his mother and grandmother instilled in him during his youth. So, based on their dedication to God's Word, the principle we discover is this: *A balanced woman sees Scripture as vital, representing God's authoritative Word and will for her life.*

Every day, the world washes over women's minds a tide of images and opinions that could pull them into a sea of confusion. God's Word is like a breakwater that keeps them safely within His harbor of truth. Particularly today, it is crucial for women to remain committed to studying the Scriptures.

Concerning Herself

The next person we'll visit is Lydia, a businesswoman Paul met while preaching in Philippi.

> And a certain woman named Lydia, from the city of Thyatira, a seller of purple fabrics, a worshiper of God, was listening; and the Lord opened her heart to respond to the things spoken by Paul. And when she and her household had been baptized, she urged us, saying, "If you have judged me to be faithful to

57

the Lord, come into my house and stay." And she prevailed upon us. (Acts 16:14–15)

Do you notice someone missing in these verses? Where's Lydia's husband? Perhaps he had died or had left her. Wherever he was, by encouraging "her household" to be baptized, Lydia showed a strong, guiding hand in her family's spiritual life. She also demonstrated assertiveness when she "urged" and "prevailed upon" Paul and his companions to center the church in her house. An industrious and devout woman, Lydia exemplified confidence and leadership.

Another woman with similar characteristics is Priscilla, Aquila's wife and co-minister. Paul found them in Corinth and enlisted their help in that fledgling church. They then accompanied him to Ephesus, where they stayed to parent the church on their own for a while. In Paul's absence, Apollos, a gifted speaker, began teaching; but his theology was incomplete.

> When Priscilla and Aquila heard him, they took him aside and explained to him the way of God more accurately. (18:26b)

Aquila *and* Priscilla corrected his theology, and Apollos welcomed their instruction. Paul also acknowledged their valuable ministry in his letter to the Romans, referring to them as "my fellow workers in Christ Jesus" (Rom. 16:3b).

Think about this for a moment. Both a church leader and an apostle respected this woman's theological insight and allowed her to confidently use her gifts in the Lord's work. Along with Lydia, Priscilla teaches us an important principle: *A balanced woman sees herself as valuable, gifted, and responsible for her own growth toward maturity.*

Concerning the Lord

The last women we'll glean insights from are the four daughters of Philip the evangelist. Paul met them as he was preparing to return to Jerusalem—a city not friendly toward the Apostle.

> On the next day we left and came to Caesarea, and entering the house of Philip the evangelist, who was one of the seven, we stayed with him. Now this man had four virgin daughters who were prophetesses. (Acts 21:8–9)

Many people had been warning Paul not to go to Jerusalem

because the Jews there might arrest him. The prophet Agabus even dramatized Paul's inevitable imprisonment by binding his own hands and feet with Paul's belt, saying,

> "'In this way the Jews at Jerusalem will bind the man who owns this belt and deliver him into the hands of the Gentiles.'" (v. 11b)

Hearing this bleak prediction, Paul's friends "as well as the local residents began begging him not to go up to Jerusalem" (v. 12). We can assume that the four prophetesses were among this group. Convinced Paul was making a mistake, they could have pushed or bargained or tried to manipulate him into changing his mind. But, apparently, when Paul refused to heed their advice, they quietly accepted the Lord's will for him.

Their humble reaction teaches us a final truth: *A balanced woman of God sees the Lord as her refuge and buffer when things refuse to work out right.*

Three Practical Suggestions

It's one thing to draw out these principles from Scripture; it's another to hold them up to our lips and taste them. Here are three suggestions to help you drink in these truths.

First, *become a serious student of Scripture.* Romance novels and daytime television dramas tantalize many women with forbidden love and juicy intrigue. But these images only serve to pollute our minds. Our thoughts remain cleaner and our relationships clearer when we meditate on the pure wisdom of Scripture.

Second, *guard against the extremes.* The militant mentality lacks tolerance and wisdom, while the passive, helpless role lacks maturity. Neither is supported in Scripture, so avoid both of them.

Third, *commit yourself to working through conflicts rather than running from them.* Be willing to talk things through. Help your spouse and children understand that your life doesn't merely revolve around meeting their needs. Don't give in just to keep the peace, but stand strong in your value as a person and in the contribution you make. And don't be intimidated by the world's superwoman ideal —be yourself, the way God created you to be. That's all God expects.

Living Insights

For Women Only (Part One)

Meet your competition—the television advertiser's perfect woman. She's a well-dressed, well-educated, physically fit, self-fulfilled, career woman/PTA president/mother who has given natural birth to two environmentally sensitive children and is married to an admiring husband. There she goes, striding across your TV screen, full of confidence and buoyant energy.

The Bionic Woman couldn't live up to that ideal! Do you remember Lindsay Wagner in the television show *The Bionic Woman?* She could jump off a two-story building, run like a cheetah, hear a whisper at two hundred yards, and bend an iron bar. But put her in a room with three preschoolers all day or send her to work in a dingy office; then tell her to cook dinner, clean the house, and do the laundry. How long do you think she would last?

Still, many women try to compete with the world's ideal of perfection. Have you been burdening yourself with these kinds of unrealistic expectations? List a few of them.

_____

_____

_____

Thankfully, God's expectations are different than the world's. He simply asks you to be yourself, the way He created you. Isn't that a freeing thought? If you've been trying to do it all and have it all, maybe you need to adjust your expectations. Take some time to realistically determine your unique God-given abilities and character qualities. What are they?

_____   _____

_____   _____

_____   _____

In what specific ways do you feel society and the media devalue these good traits?

_____

Now jot down a promise to yourself that you will be who God created you to be and that you won't try to compete with Madison Avenue's perfect woman.

 Living Insights

For Women Only (Part Two)

Take a look at the magazines and books by your nightstand, and think about the television shows you've been watching. Do you sometimes wish your life was like those you read about and watch? Has this affected your attitude toward yourself and your family? How?

Have you been making decisions lately based more on secular wisdom than God's wisdom? If so, in what ways?

To be sure, many secular magazines and books broaden our thinking and build up our spirit. But many advocate an unbiblical way of life. Consider the first principle we stated in the lesson: *A balanced woman sees Scripture as vital, representing God's authoritative Word and will for her life.* Instead of flipping on the television, flip open the Bible. See what direction His Word will take you this week.

Digging Deeper

Contrary to some popular teaching about biblical submission, the Bible never portrays women as silent shadows who have little to contribute mentally or spiritually. In fact, women played an important role in Jesus' ministry and in the spread of Christianity. The following list chronicles just a few of the valuable spiritual contributions women have made in the history of the church.

Some Women in the New Testament

- Mary and Martha were close friends of Jesus.   Luke 10:38–39
- Mary anointed Jesus prior to His death.   John 12:3
- Many women lamented Jesus' crucifixion.   Luke 23:27–31; John 19:25
- The women visited Jesus' tomb on Resurrection morning.   Luke 23:55–24:1
- Early church leaders responded positively to widows' complaints.   Acts 6:1–6
- Dorcas was "abounding with deeds of kindness and charity" throughout her community. When Peter later raised her from the dead, many townspeople believed in Christ.   Acts 9:36–42
- The church gathered in Mary's home to pray for Peter.   Acts 12:12
- Women gathered for worship at Philippi, where Paul spoke to them.   Acts 16:13
- Lydia was a successful businesswoman. She became a Christian and prevailed upon Paul and his colleagues to meet in her home.   Acts 16:14–15
- In Thessalonica "a number of the leading women" were responsive to Paul and Silas' teaching.   Acts 17:4
- In Berea "many . . . believed, along with a number of prominent Greek women."   Acts 17:12
- In Athens some believed, including Damaris.   Acts 17:34

- Priscilla with her husband Aquila were partners in church work. — Acts 18:2–3, 18–19
- Both Priscilla and Aquila helped hone Apollos' theology. — Acts 18:26
- Paul called Priscilla and Aquila his "fellow workers." — Romans 16:3
- Paul mentioned Phoebe as "a servant of the church . . . a helper of many, and of myself as well." — Romans 16:1–2
- "Chloe's people" gave Paul information on the Corinthian problems. — 1 Corinthians 1:11
- Widows were given special attention, assistance, and care. — 1 Timothy 5:3–16
- Older women were instructed to "encourage" younger women. — Titus 2:3–4
- Apphia is called "our sister" in Paul's letter to Philemon. — Philemon 2
- The second letter of John was addressed to "the chosen lady." — 2 John 1

Chapter 8

BEYOND CHARM
AND BEAUTY
Proverbs 31:10–31

Rather than praise wives and mothers for their invaluable role in society, the world often promises a more glamorous life outside that role—a life that is usually more shadow than substance. One of Aesop's fables, "The Dog and the Shadow," warns of what might happen if we pursue this illusion.

> A Dog had stolen a piece of meat out of a butcher's shop, and was crossing a river on its way home, when he saw his own shadow reflected in the stream below. Thinking that it was another dog with another piece of meat, he resolved to make himself master of that also, but in snapping at the supposed treasure he dropped the bit he was carrying, which immediately sank to the bottom and was irrecoverably lost.
>
> Application: Grasp at the shadow and lose the substance.[1]

We chuckle at the greedy dog who gets what he deserves; but consider for a moment the women who have lost the substance of their lives while grasping at shadows—the wife who has traded her marriage for an illusory morsel of forbidden love, or the mother who has lost her children along the way to a prestigious career. Solomon observed the marked contrast between the woman who holds onto substance and the one who darts after shadows:

> The wise woman builds her house,
> But the foolish tears it down with her own hands.
> (Prov. 14:1)

If you are a wife or mother, we want to affirm the tangible treasure in your grasp. God says your role is significant and worthy of honor. According to Proverbs, "An excellent wife is the crown

---

1. Artzybasheff, Boris, ed. and ill. *Aesop's Fables* (New York, N.Y.: Viking Press, 1933), p. 46.

of her husband" (12:4a), and a faithful mother is worthy of her family's praise (31:28–29).

In this chapter, we'll take a look at that faithful woman portrayed in Proverbs 31. Her example reveals a treasure chest of gems that outshine any shadows women might be tempted to chase. Let's open this cache together and discover the riches God has given each woman to enjoy.

General Overview

This treatise on the excellent wife is the grand finale of the book of Proverbs. The fact that it occupies this place of honor is a tribute in itself to the significance of women. Interestingly, verses 10–31 form an acrostic—the first letters of the twenty-two verses comprise, in consecutive order, the twenty-two letters in the Hebrew alphabet. Doubtless, it was written this way to help people remember the qualities young women should aspire to and young men should look for in a wife.

According to verse 1, this passage was passed down to the author, King Lemuel, from his mother. Tradition identifies this man as King Solomon. If that is correct, the woman who originated these wise words was Bathsheba—David's wife by scandal (see 2 Sam. 11:1 12:25). This fact gives hope to any woman who thinks her past invalidates her from excelling in godliness later in life.

The woman portrayed in Proverbs 31:10–31 gracefully models three gems that all wives and mothers hold within their grasp.

What a Woman Holds within Her Grasp

Following the author's descriptions, let's observe how this woman displays these precious possessions.

Her Value before God

First, we notice that the passage begins and ends proclaiming her exquisite value:

> An excellent wife, who can find?
> For her worth is far above jewels. (v. 10)

> "Many daughters have done nobly,
> But you excel them all."
> Charm is deceitful and beauty is vain,

But a woman who fears the Lord, she shall be
praised. (vv. 29–30)

Several facets of her value shimmer in the light. She is so rare,
not many can find her. She is worth more than the Hope diamond.
Her inner character eclipses both beauty and charm. And she "fears
the Lord"—she reveres Him and loves Him.

Her Role as a Wife

Also within this woman's grasp was the significance of her role
as a wife. According to the world, the title "wife" conjures up images
of a weary and unappreciated Cinderella, fetching coal and scrub-
bing floors. But notice the respect given this wife:

The heart of her husband trusts in her,
And he will have no lack of gain.
She does him good and not evil
All the days of her life. (vv. 11–12)

Because of her godly character, her husband trusts her. He has
confidence in her, believes in her, and values her judgment. She,
on the other hand, "does him good," benefits him, and encourages
him to succeed. She finds delight in his work and responsibilities.

Some wives do evil to their husbands by needling them with
critical remarks or manipulating them to get their way. History's
first wife, Eve, gave Adam the fruit forbidden by God; Solomon's
idol-worshiping wives stole his heart away from God; and the
woman who symbolizes feminine treachery, Jezebel, assisted Ahab
in all kinds of evil.

But the wife in Proverbs 31 brings out the best in her husband;
in turn, he praises her (see vv. 28–29). Consequently, she has what
many wives and mothers lack, a high self-esteem.

Strength and dignity are her clothing,
And she smiles at the future. (v. 25)

Sadly, instead of being clothed in the flowing robes of strength
and dignity, many women today look in the mirror and see themselves draped in the tattered rags of self-doubt and shame. Why do
they have such a low view of themselves? James Dobson provides
one reason:

If women felt genuinely respected in their role as
wives and mothers, they would not need to abandon

66

it for something better. If they felt *equal* with men in personal worth, they would not need to be equivalent to men in responsibility. If they could only bask in the dignity and status granted them by the Creator, then their femininity would be valued as their greatest asset, rather than scorned as an old garment to be discarded. Without question, the future of a nation depends on how it sees its women, and I hope we will teach our little girls to be glad they were chosen by God for the special pleasures of womanhood.[2]

Husbands and children, nothing thrills the heart of your wives and mothers like your praise. She longs for it. Like a flower on a parched landscape, she drinks it in. Do not deprive her soul of the nourishment it needs and unwittingly send her searching for fulfillment elsewhere.

Her Characteristics in the Home, Household, and Community

The many facets of her character comprise the final gem the Proverbs 31 woman possesses as a wife and mother. Even the casual reader will be struck by her industriousness.

> She looks for wool and flax,
> And works with her hands in delight.
> She is like merchant ships;
> She brings her food from afar.
> She rises also while it is still night,
> And gives food to her household,
> And portions to her maidens. (vv. 13–15)

Whew! She wears us out just reading about her. But then, what modern wife and mother doesn't have an equally long list of accomplishments, including working in and out of the home, piloting the family ship through sickness and job loss, and bringing "her food from afar" at the best bargains possible. All this she does with a gracious, thoughtful attitude.

Shrewd wisdom is another characteristic of the woman in Proverbs 31. With her money, she invests in property and "plants a

2. James Dobson, *What Wives Wish Their Husbands Knew about Women* (Wheaton, Ill.: Tyndale House Publishers, 1975), p. 35.

vineyard" (v. 16). Through her self-confidence, she displays strength of spirit (v. 17). In the next verse, the phrase "Her lamp does not go out at night" means that her home is a haven for the distressed (v. 18b).[3] She is compassionate and caring.

> She extends her hand to the poor,
> And she stretches out her hands to the needy.
> She is not afraid of the snow for her household,
> For all her household are clothed with scarlet.
> (vv. 20–21)

She reaches beyond the needs of her family and her circle of friends to include those on the outside. Even the way she dresses reveals an air of dignity (v. 22). She recognizes her husband's importance but does not hide behind his shadow (vv. 23–24). And she is sensitive to her children's needs:

> She opens her mouth in wisdom,
> And the teaching of kindness is on her tongue.
> She looks well to the ways of her household,
> And does not eat the bread of idleness.
> Her children rise up and bless her;
> Her husband also, and he praises her, saying:
> "Many daughters have done nobly,
> But you excel them all." (vv. 26–29)

Now, as a wife and mother, you're probably saying, "My kids only rise up and bless me when they want something; and if my husband said those words to me, I'd probably wonder if he was feeling all right!"

Before you push this passage aside as being unrealistic, think about the ways you really do resemble the Proverbs 31 woman. Because of you, your family probably eats well, don't they? They have clothes to wear and a comfortable home to live in. You're probably good at finding bargains. You're certainly wiser than you were a few years ago. Your children learn valuable lessons about life from you. Don't underestimate yourself! Your family needs you to

---

3. According to Jeanne W. Hendricks, "In the ancient East, a lamp burned in the home of citizens of means to signify their availability. Here was a haven for the distressed. The old Bedouins had a saying, 'He sleeps in darkness,' which conveyed the idea of living in abject poverty. A burning candle signified prosperity." *A Woman for All Seasons* (Nashville, Tenn.: Thomas Nelson, Publishers, 1977), p. 181.

touch them, to hold them, to give them worth and purpose, dignity and discipline . . . and best of all, your love.

Conclusion

Because you are a wife and a mother, you have in your grasp the same admirable qualities the Proverbs 31 woman possessed so long ago. Here are some questions that will encourage you to never let them go.

First, *do you find yourself attracted more to the shadows than to the substance?* If so, think before you leap.

Second, *are you convinced of your value in God's eyes?* Don't let lack of praise from society or your children or husband feed you the lie that you are not valuable. Learn to see yourself the way God sees you.

Third, *have you been challenged by the character traits listed in Proverbs 31?* Perhaps you've been trying to impress the world and have lacked wisdom or confidence. Maybe you've been focusing your energies on less important tasks. Or, possibly, you need to work on building a positive, generous attitude. Ask the Lord to make these qualities real in your life.

Fourth, *husbands and children, do you see the value of your wife and mother?* Protect your home against the intrusion of a critical spirit that would steal her self-confidence. Praise her strength and dignity. Affirm her calling. Point out the good things she does. Return to her the fruit she produces in you. Serve as she serves and love as she loves.

> Give her the product of her hands,
> And let her works praise her in the gates. (v. 31)

Living Insights

For Husbands Only

Enter the king. He's come home after a day of battling bosses and deadlines. Wearily, he opens the castle door and is welcomed by his adoring queen . . . who's more frazzled than he is. A pot on the stove is boiling over, the cartoon video is blaring, the kids have tied the dog to the canary cage, and her highness, who hasn't had even a two-minute break to brush her hair, is mopping up another spilled glass of juice.

Probably at this moment, the king's words to his queen are not going to overflow with praise. In fact, if the king is like many husbands, his primary concern is more self-preservation than praising his hard-working wife. Yet his encouragement is an essential building block to her emotional health. His words can uplift her spirit or tear it down.

Can simple words really make that much difference in a person's life?

Yes. To illustrate, consider the story of Aldonza in the play *Man of La Mancha*. She knows nothing of real love, only the harsh reality of the abusive men who take advantage of her. Despising herself and the life she leads, she feels dirty and cheap . . . until she meets Don Quixote.

He is an aging gentleman, gone insane with a dream to bring justice and gallantry back into the world. In his harmless delusion, he sees people not as they are but as they are meant to be. When he first catches sight of the ragged Aldonza, he doesn't leer like the other men; he calls her his lady, Dulcinea—his sweet one.

By merely changing her name, Don Quixote communicates her infinite value, treating her with dignity and respect. She begins to see herself as he does, and it changes her life.

Do you see your wife as she appears on the surface or as God means her to be? He calls her by a very special name:

> See how great a love the Father has bestowed
> upon us, that we should be called children of God;
> and such we are. (1 John 3:1a)

She is a child of the King. Do you treat her like royalty? Do you commend her for all she does for you and the family? The next time you come home from work, try bringing with you a few words of praise.

Living Insights

For Children Only

Imagine discovering an abandoned farmhouse along a lonely country road. Shrouding the house in a tangle of branches are the shade trees its owner planted years ago. One fir tree sags low, almost obscuring the weathered front door. Inside, the wooden floors, stiff with age, groan with every footstep as you walk through the halls.

All the rooms are dark and musty, except one. At the far corner of the house, the kitchen glows in warm, golden tones. You get the feeling that, at any moment, someone will return through the back door, arms loaded with fresh vegetables.

All points of family life once converged in this room, and it is fitting that here the mother's touch is still evident. The peeling, daisied wallpaper invites you to sit and talk. The smell of warm bread lingers in the air. The wind whistles the tunes the mother once sang, and you can almost see her dabbing her child's scraped knee or comforting her teenager's broken heart. More than just a kitchen, this was her clinic, her counseling room, her place of business.

Eventually, the trees will enfold the old house, causing it to collapse in a heap of rotting wood. But in the minds of certain children, the memory of their mother and her qualities of diligence and love will stay forever fixed. Through the years, houses and kitchens have changed dramatically. The microwave now cooks our favorite foods, and automatic gadgets save us time and work. But mothers themselves really haven't changed. They're still as inviting and tender as they always were.

Won't you tell your mother how much she means to you? Soon?

Chapter 9

A VOTE IN FAVOR OF FATHERHOOD

Selected Scriptures

In a typical Mother's Day sermon, preachers usually shower moms with bouquets of praise. But what happens on Father's Day? Those same preachers often turn and wallop dads with fistfuls of convicting exhortations. It's enough to make dads gun-shy when it comes to the subject of fatherhood. The Bible, though, actually speaks highly of fathers. For instance, in the book of Proverbs all twenty-six references to fathers paint them in a positive light.

Now, we know that fathers aren't perfect. And they know it too, though they're sometimes afraid to admit their faults. However, rather than harping on their failures, wouldn't it be healthier to point out what we appreciate about our dads?

Solomon could have been bitter toward his father, David, because of his many failings. Yet he writes from his heart, "The glory of sons is their fathers" (Prov. 17:6b). Despite David's shortcomings, Solomon gloried in his father's character qualities. Let's look at some of the proverbs that illustrate those qualities and, in so doing, cast our vote—along with Solomon—in favor of fatherhood.

Casting a Vote in Favor of Their Roles

Let's begin by affirming fathers for the roles they fill in the home.

Provider

Two references in Proverbs highlight dads in their role as the family provider.

> House and wealth are an inheritance from fathers. (19:14a)

> A good man leaves an inheritance to his children's children. (13:22a)

Think of the long hours a father spends grinding out a living, perhaps at a job he doesn't enjoy. Think of the pounding headaches caused by demanding bosses, dreary traveling, stress, and sore muscles. For what? A paycheck that disappears as soon as he brings it home. Because of his sacrifices, though, the family has a place to live, food to eat, clothes to wear, and maybe a little money left over for fun. And if he's a good planner, even his grandchildren will reap the benefits of his labor through an inheritance.

Maintainer

Another proverb describes the father's role as the family maintainer. This verse refers to the Hebrew practice of marking property lines that subsequent generations were to respect.

> Do not move the ancient boundary
> Which your fathers have set. (22:28)

In those days, the father's job was to maintain the boundaries that bordered his family's land. Today's fathers, though, rather than building walls of stone, establish boundaries of morality and integrity. They set the limits on acceptable behavior.

Young people, of course, tend to push against those limits. But the truth is, they feel most secure when their fathers keep the boundaries intact. Deep down, kids are searching for role models who stand by what they believe. And there's no hero your child wants more than you, Dad. That doesn't mean you have to be perfect. You'll find that if you can say, "I'm sorry; I was wrong," your children will forgive you and respect you for being honest.

Instructor

The third role in which Solomon sees fathers is that of instructor. Out of his pen flow several proverbs expressing the value of a father's wise counsel.

> Hear, my son, your father's instruction,
> And do not forsake your mother's teaching;
> Indeed, they are a graceful wreath to your head,
> And ornaments about your neck. (1:8–9)

> Hear, O sons, the instruction of a father,
> And give attention that you may gain
>   understanding,
> For I give you sound teaching;
> Do not abandon my instruction.
> When I was a son to my father,
> Tender and the only son in the sight of my mother,

Then he taught me and said to me,
"Let your heart hold fast my words;
Keep my commandments and live;
Acquire wisdom! Acquire understanding!
Do not forget, nor turn away from the words of
 my mouth." (4:1–5)

My son, observe the commandment of your
 father,
And do not forsake the teaching of your mother;
Bind them continually on your heart;
Tie them around your neck.
When you walk about, they will guide you;
When you sleep, they will watch over you;
And when you awake, they will talk to you.
(6:20–22)

As a teenager, you probably rolled your eyes when your dad started another one of his lectures. Later, though, when you were on your own, his corny sayings suddenly became pearls of wisdom, and his compliments that used to embarrass you in front of your friends became coveted encouragements. His advice about choosing the right friends, keeping your word, and doing your best really came in handy, didn't it? Maybe your father even helped you relate to the opposite sex and warned you about the dangers of immorality. Solomon describes the priceless treasure of that kind of instruction:

For the commandment is a lamp and the
 teaching is light;
And reproofs for discipline are the way of life,
To keep you from the evil woman,
From the smooth tongue of the adulteress.
Do not desire her beauty in your heart,
Nor let her capture you with her eyelids.
(6:23–25)

Words like these are not easy to give or receive, but in them is life. And for them, we say, "Thanks, Dad."

The other side of a father's role as instructor is his role as forgiver. Perhaps you can recall ignoring your dad's instructions and facing the consequences of your disobedience. Afterward, did he affirm you with an understanding hug or reassuring smile? That act of forgiveness was like hanging an ornament of grace around your neck and is a vital aspect of fatherhood. Without it, anger can begin to boil inside a child's heart. Paul warns:

> Fathers, do not provoke your children to anger, but bring them up in the discipline and instruction of the Lord. (Eph. 6:4)

Commentator William Hendriksen identifies six ways fathers can provoke their children to anger:

1. Overprotection

2. Favoritism

3. Discouragement

4. Failure to make allowance for the child's individuality, opinions, and growth

5. Neglect

6. Bitter words and outright physical cruelty[1]

A more constructive course of action, according to Paul, is to *nourish* your children—which is the literal meaning of the Greek word translated "bring them up" (v. 4b). *Discipline* means "education" in its broader sense, and it includes the ideas of chastening and correcting (see also Heb. 12:5–11). *Instruction* emphasizes "training by means of the spoken word, whether that word be teaching, warning, or encouragement."[2] This kind of instruction doesn't mean hammering the truth into your children through fist-waving lectures. Rather, as a result of spending time with your kids, you instruct by imparting wisdom naturally as each situation unfolds.

Casting a Vote in Favor of Their Relationships

Looking at a few more of Solomon's proverbs, we also learn from fathers' relationships, first to their wives.

With the Mother of Their Children

The greatest gift a father gives his children is his affection for their mother. By wrapping his arms around his wife, he enfolds

---

1. See William Hendriksen, *New Testament Commentary: Exposition of Ephesians* (Grand Rapids, Mich.: Baker Book House, 1967), pp. 261–62.

2. Hendriksen, *Exposition of Ephesians*, p. 262.

them in a blanket of trust and security as well. Solomon speaks candidly to husbands about the importance of staying faithful to their wives.

> Drink water from your own cistern
> And fresh water from your own well.
> Should your springs be dispersed abroad,
> Streams of water in the streets?
> Let them be yours alone
> And not for strangers with you.
> Let your fountain be blessed,
> And rejoice in the wife of your youth.
> As a loving hind and a graceful doe,
> Let her breasts satisfy you at all times;
> Be exhilarated always with her love.
> (Prov. 5:15–19)

These verses brim with a husband's delight in and romantic affection for his wife. Fathers, don't be afraid to demonstrate your feelings for your wife in front of the children. They'll love you both all the more.

With the Children of Their Wife

Second, we cast a vote in favor of fathers' relationships with their children.

> The father of the righteous will greatly rejoice,
> And he who begets a wise son will be glad in
>   him. (23:24)

Dads can reap a harvest of joy in their homes if they cultivate wisdom in their children. And that requires a father to get close to his children—so close that his character qualities rub off on them, which is a father's greatest cause for rejoicing.

One Last Word

There is one more special ingredient to invest in your child: integrity.

> A righteous man who walks in his integrity—
> How blessed are his sons after him. (20:7)

Bruce Lockerbie, in an excellent book called *Fatherlove*, gives us a picture of the blessing a father can leave behind.

> When I was just eleven years old, our family drove from Toronto to Eastern Ontario, to the region north of the St. Lawrence River, where my father had been born. We reached the little villages of Ventnor and Spencerville just before midnight; the residents had long since gone to bed. But Dad needed directions to find the old homestead, where we were to spend the night. Reluctantly he stopped at a darkened house and knocked on the door. After several minutes of waiting, the yard light came on, and an older man opened his door. I could hear my father apologizing for the inconvenience; then he identified himself as the son of Pearson Lockerbie— my grandfather dead for more than a score of years.
> "Come in, come in," said the man. "No trouble at all. We knew your father."
> That's the greatest legacy a man can leave his son.[3]

Will those who know you and outlive you be quick to open their homes to your children? Are you cultivating that kind of legacy?

Living Insights

For Fathers Only

"I'd love to help you build the model airplane, Son. After I mow the lawn."

"After I clean up the garage."

"After a little nap, OK?"

"I'll help you, I promise. First, I have to run to the store."

"Oh no! I forgot about tonight's board meeting. Son, we'll put the airplane together tomorrow . . . after church."

All fathers wish they could spend more time with their children. But work takes time, chores take time, church takes time, and unfortunately, children get the leftovers. It's difficult to fill the role of "instructor," though, when the pupils and the teacher hardly ever get together. What's the solution?

3. D. Bruce Lockerbie, *Fatherlove: Learning to Give the Best You've Got* (Garden City, N.Y.: Doubleday and Co., 1981), pp. 234–35.

Give the leftovers to someone else for a while.

In the following space, take a few moments to plan time for you and your children. Put everything else on hold. Tell the boss you can't stay late that evening. Tell the grass and weeds that they'll just have to wait. Ask someone else to handle your church responsibilities. You're going to spend quality *and* quantity time with your children. You have a model airplane to build!

_____

_____

_____

_____

 ## Living Insights

After concluding his speech to generous applause, columnist D. L. Stewart drove home with his impressed fourteen-year-old son.

> "I really admire you, Dad, being able to get up there and give a speech like that. You always know what to say to people. You always seem to know what you're doing."
>
> I smiled when he said that. I may even have blushed modestly. But, at that moment, I didn't know what to say at all.
>
> After a while I thanked him and assured him that some day he would be comfortable speaking in front of an audience, that he would always know what to say to people, that he would always know what he was doing. But what I really wanted to say to my son was that his father was not at all what he appeared to be and that being a man is frequently a facade. . . .
>
> It's different for fathers than it is for mothers. Motherhood is honest, close to the surface. Mothers don't have to hide what they feel. They don't have to pretend.
>
> When there are sounds downstairs in the middle of the night, a mother is allowed to pull the covers

over her head and hope that they will go away. A father is supposed to put on his slippers and robe and march boldly down the stairs, even if he's pretty sure that it's the Manson family waiting for him in the kitchen.

When the road signs are confusing and the scenery is starting to look awfully unfamiliar, it's perfectly natural for a mother to pull over to the side of the road and ask for directions from the first person who comes along. A father is supposed to know exactly where he's going, even if he has to drive 200 miles out of the way to prove it.

When the electricity goes out, no one questions a mother who simply lights a few candles and waits for the repairman to get there. But everyone wonders about a father who doesn't pick up a screwdriver and head for the basement, even though he doesn't know his fuse box from his sump pump.

Mothers can load a broken bike into the rear of the station wagon and drive it to the repair shop. Fathers are supposed to be able to fix it on the spot.

Mothers can sit in the stands at a football game and cover their eyes and worry that it's their kid who's going to be dragged out from underneath the pile of players with his arm broken in eight places. The father's job is to pace the sidelines and shout, "Let's hit somebody out there, Son," and never let anyone know that he holds his breath everytime the pile winds up on top of his kid.

Mothers can admit to the real estate agent that they don't know a thing about fixed-rate interest and balloon payments and second mortgages. Fathers are supposed to nod their heads and pretend that it all makes perfect sense.

Mothers can bang a new jar of peanut butter on the floor until the lid is loose enough to turn. Fathers are supposed to twist it off with their bare hands— without getting red in the face.

Mothers who lose their jobs are unfortunate. Fathers who lose their jobs are failures. . . .

I should have told him that the only reason his

father, like lots of fathers, doesn't admit his weaknesses is because he is afraid that someone will think he is not a real man.

More important, what I should have said to my 14-year-old son in the car that night is that someday, when he's a father, he'll feel fear and self-doubt and pain, and that it's all right. But my father never told me, and I haven't told my son.[4]

Dads, did your father ever tell you that it's all right? What will you tell your sons?

4. D. L. Stewart, "Why Fathers Hide Their Feelings," *Redbook*, January 1985, p. 32.

Chapter 10

TOP TEMPTATIONS
FATHERS FACE
Selected Scriptures

For many fathers, there's nothing that will bring out their best like the vivid realization of how much their children's lives and futures depend on them. Chuck Swindoll discovered this in a gripping, unforgettable way.

> I remember the time I came closer to drowning than ever in my life. I had one of our children on my shoulders—we were up at Lake Tahoe. And while holding this precious child, I thought it would be neat to wade into the cold waters. I stepped in and noticed right away that the bank was unusually soft and muddy. I went on, knowing that it could be a little dangerous and slippery, so I wanted to be careful not to go too deep.
>
> As I walked along with my child on my shoulders, I thought, Well, I'm in the water, I might as well get his little feet wet along with mine. So I stepped a little deeper. Before long, the water was neck deep for me, but it just covered his feet. I thought it would be fun to bob up and down a little, and as my head would go underwater, of course his would stay above the water. It would come to his waist. Oh, it was cold! And he thought this was great. And I thought, Well, if that's great, we'll just go another step. And I stepped into nothing.
>
> Understand my intolerable predicament. I cannot let go to swim because he's too young to swim and would drown. So, left with the strength of my legs, I kicked furiously. To my shock, we drifted *away* from shore. Anyone who has been to Tahoe knows how deep it gets and how quickly. And I am in the open lake, well over my head. Cynthia was onshore and out of sight, and I was literally gasping—struggling to keep my nose above water.

My son, however, thought we were still having fun! He continued slapping me on the head and laughing and kicking his feet so the water was churning up into my face. And I am seized with panic that we will not make it back alive.

I took one final gasp—part air, part water—and as I choked and spit and gagged, I suddenly realized that if I went, he went too. I could not bear the thought. Something within me gave an extra surge of energy to kick toward the shore. It was just enough for me to reach out and get a toehold on a tiny root that was growing beneath the surface. It was just enough to pull me over. I remember sloshing up on the bank of that lake and falling backwards, gasping, realizing how close I had come to disaster.[1]

As much as fathers want to do their best for their children, they still encounter forces that do everything they can to sink a dad. One of these forces is temptation, and from Chuck's frightening experience at Lake Tahoe we can cull at least three truths about the temptations fathers face.

First, they are as subtle as the muddy banks of that lake. Temptations are slick and submerged beneath life's surface, which makes them especially treacherous.

Second, temptations invite fathers to go further. Deeper and deeper a dad may go into the water, flirting with temptation and feeling confident that he can play the game and win. Suddenly, though, he loses his footing and is fighting for his life.

Third, the longer fathers play in these dangerous waters, the more threatening the situation becomes—not only for fathers but also for those sitting on their shoulders. As a result, when a father finally sinks into the murky depths of sin and its consequences, he pulls his family down with him.

What can fathers do to protect themselves—and their children —from drowning? We wish the answer was as simple as "Don't go near the water." But, according to James, dealing with temptation is more involved than that.

---

1. Adapted from a personal story related by Chuck Swindoll in his sermon titled "Top Temptations Fathers Face," given at the First Evangelical Free Church of Fullerton on June 17, 1990.

Two Realities

In the first chapter of his letter, James describes several situations in which all of us find ourselves from time to time. Sometimes we lack wisdom (v. 5); sometimes, faith (vv. 6–8). Sometimes we live humbly (v. 9); sometimes, abundantly (vv. 10–11). But there are two realities we face constantly. James addresses them in verses 12–16:

> Blessed is a man who perseveres under trial; for once he has been approved, he will receive the crown of life which the Lord has promised to those who love Him. Let no one say when he is tempted, "I am being tempted by God"; for God cannot be tempted by evil, and He Himself does not tempt anyone. But each one is tempted when he is carried away and enticed by his own lust. Then when lust has conceived, it gives birth to sin; and when sin is accomplished, it brings forth death. Do not be deceived, my beloved brethren.

We are always enduring some kind of trial, and we are always being tempted. There is no escape to higher ground, particularly in the realm of temptation. As a result, the banks will invariably be soft and slippery beneath a father's feet, ever beckoning him to wander into the deeper, dangerous parts of the lake. Safety can be found not in hoping the temptations will go away but in understanding their perilous nature and avoiding them.

So let's take some soundings of the lake bottom to see what dangers lurk offshore.

Six Temptations

The first underwater ledge drops off in the part of the lake known as material possessions.

Material Possessions

There's nothing wrong with owning things. We must have possessions in order to live, and, according to Paul, the father who doesn't supply food, clothes, and shelter for his family "is worse than an unbeliever" (1 Tim. 5:8b). While providing these things, however, a father can be tempted *to substitute what he purchases for his family for his presence with his family*. He can be tempted to give toys instead of time.

Unfortunately, his workplace oils this slippery temptation with the promise that by working more, he can buy more; and by buying more, his family will be better off. So he pours himself into his career—working weekends, traveling constantly, and doing whatever it takes to advance in the company. But Jesus warned,

> "For not even when one has an abundance does his life consist of his possessions." (Luke 12:15b)

Nothing—no *thing*—can substitute for a father's presence. Ask children what they remember most about their fathers, and you'll find that it wasn't the closet full of designer-label clothes he bought them. It was the times he tickled them when they were little, cheered for them at their ball games, or sat up waiting for them to come home at night. It was his touch, his smile, his encouragement. Far more than a nice house to live in and lots of toys to play with, children need their father's caring presence.

Emotional Strength

The second area of danger concerns a father's emotional strength. Every man has a limited supply of emotional resources that fuel his creativity, leadership, sense of humor, and enthusiasm for life. But a father is often tempted *to save his best for the workplace and give his family the leftovers*.

For example, he may rise early in the morning, jog, shower, and take off for work like a 747 zooming down the runway. At the office, he's motivated; he's innovative; he overflows with problem-solving energy. About five o'clock, though, his fuel starts running low. And by the time he lands at home in the evening, he's ready to taxi to the easy chair and shut down his engines.

It's easy for a father to fall into this routine, becoming more attentive to the needs of his coworkers than those of his wife and children. But his family requires the same strength that he gives his work, if not more. And when the weekend rolls around, it's too late to make up for his absence the rest of the week. Instead, he must learn to pace himself, to save some of his zeal and creativity for his family.

As a father, is your energy gauge on empty whenever you are home? Where are you expending your fuel? Maybe this is a good time to take a look at your priorities.

Verbal Capability

Another likely area of danger is a father's verbal capability. The temptation here is *to deliver lectures rather than earn the right to be respected through listening and learning.*

A man may be able to lecture his employees, but the home is not the office, and his wife and children are not subordinates. Fathers who order their children around will only lose the respect they hoped to gain.

James points dads down a better path:

> But everyone must be quick to hear, slow to speak and slow to anger. (James 1:19b)

It's tempting to reverse that order. For instance, imagine a typical dad discovering his expensive tools scattered across the garage floor. His first reaction is to be slow to speak, right? Not hardly! Often he's quick to anger, quick to speak, and slow to listen. But James is clear on this:

> The anger of man does not achieve the righteousness of God. (v. 20)

Instead of lecturing, a father earns much more respect by staying in control of himself and listening. And if he's open, he also may learn much more about his children.

Personal Desire

Fourth is the subtle yet slick temptation *to desire being perfect and demanding the same from the rest of the family.* Of course, there's nothing wrong with wanting to do a good job, but a father edges deeper into danger when doing a good job isn't good enough. Tom Eisenman, in his book *Temptations Men Face*, reflects on some of the characteristics common to perfectionists.

> *Perfectionists tend to think in dichotomous categories.* Everything in life is an either/or proposition. Either I am perfect or I am worthless. I am either a "great" father or I am a "bad" father. . . .
> *Perfectionists engage in minimizing and maximizing.* They tend to maximize failures and minimize successes. . . . There is this common inability to accept all that went right because the all-consuming focus is on the small thing that went wrong. . . .

> *Perfectionists set unrealistic goals for themselves and others. . . .*
>
> *Perfectionists struggle with low self-esteem. . . .*
>
> . . . When perfectionists evaluate their performance, they are really judging their personal worth.[2]

If you see yourself in this mirror, Eisenman offers some wise advice:

> Rethink what it means to be successful. It might help to remember, for instance, that a .300 hitter in baseball is a very good batter. But this average means that he gets a hit only three times in every ten times at bat. Some of us are trying to hit a home run every time we swing the bat. This is unrealistic. It will drive us crazy.[3]

It will drive our families crazy too! According to Ephesians 6:4, Paul warned: "Fathers, do not exasperate your children" (NIV). A father exasperates his kids when he expects them to get ten hits out of ten tries at bat. That kind of pressure ends up destroying creativity and true productivity—children become afraid to even step up to the plate. Fathers have to give themselves and their children room to fail.

Sexual Drive

A father's sexuality is the fifth danger zone. The temptation is for him *to seek intimate satisfaction outside the bonds of monogamy.* Plain and simple, it's the temptation to have an affair.

Let's apply James' words in verses 13–15 specifically to fathers. First, when you are tempted sexually, don't rationalize and say, "I am being tempted by God" (v. 13a). Hiding behind such statements as, "If God hadn't brought me to this hotel . . ." or, "If God hadn't caused this woman to cross my path . . ." just doesn't work. Because, as James continues, "He Himself does not tempt anyone" (v. 13b). Within God's sovereign rule, He may permit temptation, but He is not its originator.

Rather, a man "is carried away and enticed by his own lust"

---

2. Tom L. Eisenman, *Temptations Men Face* (Downers Grove, Ill.: InterVarsity Press, 1990), pp. 168–70.

3. Eisenman, *Temptations Men Face*, p. 186.

(v. 14b). The Greek word for *enticed, deleaz̄o*, refers to a "fisherman who lures his prey from its retreat and entices it by bait to his trap, hook, or net."[4] What drives us to strike temptation's bait?

> We can be hooked by temptation like a fish by a worm because we're hungry . . . hungry for the fulfillment of our physical and spiritual needs. God promises to provide for these needs, but Satan also knows about our hungers. And although he cannot force us to eat, he is a skilled angler—knowing when, where, and how to drop bait in front of us that might lure us away from God.[5]

One way God provides for a father's needs is through his family. A man is more likely to swim past Satan's bait when he knows real nourishment awaits him at home. So, dads, carry family reminders with you, such as pictures or mementos. Mention your wife and kids to the women you work with. And keep in mind the precious lives resting on your shoulders.

Spiritual Faith

Finally, a dad can be tempted in the area of his spiritual faith. The temptation is *to underestimate the importance of cultivating his family's spiritual appetite.* Our "macho" culture says men don't need religion—that it's only for women and children. Yet a father who will guide his family through dark valleys with the lamp of God's Word and blanket them with prayer is God's idea of a real man.

Of course, fathers can go to the other extreme. They can become legalistic fanatics, substituting religious verbiage for genuine faith. Do you know how to tell when a dad has slipped into this sinkhole of hypocrisy? The family stops having fun. A family that feels free to laugh and play together usually lives in an atmosphere of forgiveness and grace—the kind of atmosphere fathers, in particular, have the power to create.

---

4. Fritz Rienecker, *A Linguistic Key to the Greek New Testament*, ed. Cleon L. Rogers Jr. (Grand Rapids, Mich.: Zondervan Publishing House, Regency Reference Library, 1980), p. 723.

5. From the study guide *James: Practical and Authentic Living*, written by Lee Hough, from the Bible-teaching ministry of Charles R. Swindoll (Fullerton, Calif.: Insight for Living, 1991), p. 35.

Conclusion

Concerning these six temptations, are you dangerously close to the edge? Perhaps in one or two areas, you've already slipped in up to your waist. Or to your neck. Maybe you've slid off the ledge entirely. For the sake of the innocent one on your shoulders, keep kicking. And most important, don't be afraid to call out for help.

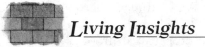 **_Living Insights_** STUDY ONE

What degree of influence do these six temptations have in your life? Write the number 1 beside the temptation that gives you the most trouble, 2 by the one giving you the second hardest time, and so on through 6.

___ I am tempted to substitute material presents for my actual presence with my family.

___ I am tempted to save my best for the workplace and give my family the leftovers.

___ I am tempted to deliver lectures rather than earn the right to be respected through listening and learning.

___ I am tempted to desire to be perfect and demand perfection from my family.

___ I am tempted to seek intimate satisfaction outside the bonds of monogamy.

___ I am tempted to underestimate the importance of cultivating my family's spiritual appetite.

Why do you think your top three temptations are the toughest to resist? Could it stem from thought patterns developed while you were growing up or from some stress you are presently enduring? Try to discover the keys.

_____

_____

_____

_____

Identifying and understanding your weaknesses are the first steps to safer footing. In the next Living Insight, we'll explore some additional ways to find your way back to shore.

Living Insights STUDY TWO

Tom Eisenman outlines a program to help men, and women too, resist temptation based on the successful twelve-step method developed by Alcoholics Anonymous. He summarizes it using the acrostic HEALED.

> Help!
> Establish your life in God
> Access accountable relationships
> List harms, repent and amend
> Enter into prayer
> Dare to share[6]

Overcoming sinful patterns is a long-term process. These steps take time to accomplish, so don't move through them hurriedly. Seriously consider each point, and go on to the next one only when you feel ready.

Help! We can't imagine someone drowning without calling out for help. With temptation, however, many people are too afraid or proud or embarrassed to admit they need a hand. Are you willing to acknowledge you have a need and to ask for help from someone you trust?

Establish your life in God. Have you drifted from the Lord? What might be keeping you from restoring your relationship with Him? He is merciful and ready to forgive. All it takes is a contrite heart to get back together with Him.

Access accountable relationships. With whom can you share your struggles? In what ways can this person keep you accountable? Write down the name of this person and what you plan to say to him or her.

_____

_____

_____

6. Eisenman, *Temptations Men Face*, p. 200.

List harms, repent, and amend. If you have succumbed to these temptations, who has been hurt by your sin? Write down their names and plan a time to apologize and ask for forgiveness.

_____

_____

_____

Enter into prayer. There is strength in prayer and meditation on Scripture. In the coming days, draw upon the Spirit's power to help you follow through with your commitments.

Dare to share. You can gain additional strength by helping those who flounder in the same waters. Don't be afraid to open your life up to others. They need what you have to offer.

Chapter 11

HOW TO MAKE
THE TRUTH "STICK"
Ezra 7:10

Have you ever wondered if teenagers' minds have a nonstick coating? For many, information tends to go in one ear, slide around without taking hold, and then slip out the other ear. That's why five minutes after explaining to a class of high school sophomores that Monday's test will cover all the United States presidents, one of the students will ask: "Are we supposed to know all these presidents for Monday's test?" It's the nonstick coating.

That's also why teens' parents worry so much. Will the spiritual truths they've been handing down for years suddenly slip out of their kids' minds when they need them most?

Using Ezra as our model, let's look at some ways young people can make the truth stick in their minds and in their lives.

Background Information

In many ways, Ezra's situation is similar to that of today's Christian teens. Having grown up in Babylon, he had just moved with his nation to study and work in Jerusalem (Ezra 7:6–8). Young people are also in transition from the familiar to the unfamiliar as they move from a protected home environment into a new world. For instance, can you recall your first few days as a freshman in high school? Like a mouse, you may have moved timidly through the crowded maze of hallways, trying to be as inconspicuous as possible. You'd heard tales of older students tormenting the freshmen and even of fights on campus. Not knowing what to expect, you remained tense and guarded. Ezra, too, was in a time of transition.

Another similarity is that Ezra was well-acquainted with God's truth: "He was a scribe skilled in the law of Moses" (v. 6a). From childhood, he had studied the Scriptures, and as a scribe, he knew them better than anyone. Many Christian young people can explain the stories of the Bible with great skill. They, too, have been taught God's Word ever since they can remember.

A final point of comparison is that Ezra walked with the Lord. Three times in chapter 7 it says that the hand of the Lord was on him (vv. 6, 9, and 28). Many Christian teens can also see the hand of the Lord on their lives. They've trusted Christ for salvation, they've been baptized, and they probably know more about the Bible than some Christian adults. God wants to cultivate that knowledge, slip His hand in theirs, and lead them in paths of ministry that only He knows. He wants all that information to stick with them and produce the fruit of wisdom as they mature in Him.

Ezra clung to his wealth of knowledge by developing four character traits—four secrets for making the truth stick that we can communicate to young people, and learn ourselves.

Secrets of Making the Truth Stick

One verse in chapter 7 unveils the secrets for us.

> For Ezra had set his heart to study the law of the Lord, and to practice it, and to teach His statutes and ordinances in Israel. (v. 10)

Let's magnify each section of this verse to examine Ezra's life in greater detail.

He Made a Personal Commitment

The first thing we notice about Ezra is that he made a personal commitment to the Lord: He "set his heart." Daniel, as a teenager, pledged himself in a similar way when he

> made up his mind that he would not defile himself with the king's choice food or with the wine which he drank. (Dan. 1:8a, emphasis added)

The Christians that God uses in powerful ways always begin their journey by making up their minds to follow Christ—even if that means sailing against the popular currents of their day. In church, floating with the Christian crowd is easy. Outside church, however, most people are moving away from God, and no Sunday school teachers or pastors are there to keep us in tow. Young people must individually make up their minds to follow the Lord—nobody else can make that decision for them. And until they make that decision, the truth will never stick.

He Became a Loyal Student of Scripture

Second, Ezra became a loyal student of Scripture, for he "set his heart to study the law of the Lord." One of the quickest ways to take the fun out of Christianity is to stop studying the Bible and rely on someone else's prepared spiritual meals. Teenagers may turn up their noses at some of Mom's dishes; but let them do their own cooking, and they'll heartily eat whatever comes out of the oven. In the same way, once they begin devouring scriptural truths on their own, the Bible tastes so much better. Studying still takes discipline, but discovering God's truths becomes more meaningful and joyful.

So help your teens read God's Word regularly, and give them a Bible they can understand and carry with them wherever they go. It is the most important gift you can buy.

He Put the Truth into Action

Third, Ezra not only studied the Scripture, he "set his heart . . . to practice it." He put the truth into action. The truth will stick when, as James advocates, young people become "doers of the word, and not merely hearers" (James 1:22). James illustrates his point:

> If anyone is a hearer of the word and not a doer, he
> is like a man who looks at his natural face in a mirror;
> for once he has looked at himself and gone away,
> he has immediately forgotten what kind of person
> he was. But one who looks intently at the perfect
> law, the law of liberty, and abides by it, not having
> become a forgetful hearer but an effectual doer, this
> man shall be blessed in what he does. (vv. 23–25)

Imagine climbing out of bed in the morning. On one side of your head, your hair is flattened smooth; on the other, it stands straight up. Your eyes are puffy, your breath would knock your dog over, and creases from your pillow are etched in your face. As you stumble into the bathroom, you flip on the light and glance in the mirror. "Aaaaagh!" But instead of brushing your hair and washing up, you turn off the light, get dressed, and inflict yourself on the world.

It's hard to believe that anyone, adult or teen, wouldn't fix the problems they see in the mirror. Yet that is what James says we do when we look into the mirror of God's Word, see all our shortcomings, but do nothing to correct them. The truth means nothing if we do not put it into practice.

He Shared What He Learned with Others

Ezra's fourth secret for making the truth stick was setting his heart "to teach [God's] statutes and ordinances in Israel" (Ezra 7:10b). In other words, he shared what he learned.

One of the best ways to learn a subject is to teach it to someone else, because you then have to look at it from a completely different perspective. Encouraging young people to share what they've learned causes them to think through their views of God one step at a time. They have to confirm whether their hearts believe what their mouths are saying. They may think they know what Christianity is all about, but not until they share their knowledge does it anchor itself in their lives.

A Final Word

We recognize that trying to help young people absorb God's truth can be frustrating. Sometimes they can appear disinterested, uncaring, and ungrateful. As a result, many parents and teachers are afraid—afraid their love and teaching will escape from their teens' lives without producing any fruit. If you have felt that fear, God puts a comforting arm around you. "Your toil is not in vain in the Lord," writes the apostle Paul (1 Cor. 15:58b). And through the prophet Isaiah, the Lord has given you a promise:

> "For as the rain and the snow come down from
>   heaven,
> And do not return there without watering the
>   earth,
> And making it bear and sprout,
> And furnishing seed to the sower and bread to
>   the eater;
> So will My word be which goes forth from My
>   mouth;
> It shall not return to Me empty,
> Without accomplishing what I desire,
> And without succeeding in the matter for which
>   I sent it." (Isa. 55:10–11)

Your teens' minds may seem as slick as ice; but God's truth, like a branch flung out on a frozen lake, will eventually sink in when the pressures of growing up begin melting their resistance. When least expected, they'll come back to you and say, "I want you to know that when you thought I didn't care, I did. When you didn't know I was interested, I was. And now that I've gone through some tough times, I want to thank you for showing me the truth."

When that happens, it will have been worth it all.

Living Insights

Young people are skillful imitators, and they don't even know it! Have you ever mistaken a teenaged son who answers the phone for his father? Or have you marveled at how similarly a maturing daughter smiles and laughs like her mother?

In the same way that young people unknowingly mimic their parents' behavior, they often follow their parents' spiritual example as well. Before challenging your teenaged son or daughter with the four secrets we described in the lesson, take a moment to measure your own life by them.

- Have you made a personal commitment to walk with the Lord?

- Have you become a loyal student of Scripture?

- Are you putting God's truth into action?

- Are you sharing what you've learned with others?

To which of these questions can you answer unhesitatingly, "Yes!" In what ways can you model that spiritual secret before your teenager?

_____

_____

_____

_____

_____

If your Christian life consists of attending church on Sunday and saying grace before dinner, that may be your kids' only perception of what it means to be a Christian. Let them know that following Christ is richer than that. And tell them by what you do, not just by what you say.

Let's get personal about putting the truth into practice by looking at an issue both adults and teens struggle with: cheating. Whether in business or in school, when we take credit for work that is not our own, we're lying. Scripture is absolutely clear about that: "Do not lie to one another" (Col. 3:9a).

For students, the temptation to cheat can be overwhelming. One respected Bible scholar, R. C. Sproul, tells his story in his book *Pleasing God.*

> I am ashamed to recount an incident in which I was involved in college. I had a friend who had great difficulty with the study of Greek. Before every test we met together and I tutored him rigorously to help him get ready. He was barely passing as we came down to the wire, the final exam. During the final exam the professor left the room, leaving us on our "honor." We did not act in an honorable way.
>
> My friend was seated next to me. As he got farther into the exam his anxiety increased. He began to crane his neck to look at my paper. I helped him. I pushed my paper to the side of my desk so that he could get a clear view of it. I was obviously a willing accomplice in the deed.
>
> When the exam grades were posted on the professor's office door, two grades were conspicuously absent. There was an asterisk next to my name and my friend's, with a note to "see the professor." My heart was pounding as I knocked on the professor's door.
>
> The professor ushered me into his office. To my sick astonishment he produced a chart of every answer of every student to every question. The chart revealed that on several questions two people and only two people had the same wrong answer. The evidence was incontrovertible. The professor looked at me sadly and said, "I have just one question for you." "Yes, sir?" I replied. "Are the answers on your paper your own?" I replied, "Yes, but—" I started to confess my complicity in the scandal. He cut me off

in mid-sentence.

"I don't want to hear it," the professor said. "All I want to know is, are your answers your own?" Again I said, "Yes," and he promptly dismissed me.

For reasons I do not understand but for which I am still grateful, the professor gave me no penalties. I received his utter mercy. My friend did not fare so well. He received an F for the entire course. The results were an academic disaster for him.

We both cheated. My help was motivated simply by compassion for his panic. I know that I took pride in his achievement because I was coaching him. I was cheating as much for me as I was for him. Either way we were being dishonest. I resolved from that day never to cheat on an exam in any way.[1]

R. C. Sproul's experience is not uncommon. Even the "good" kids who attend Christian schools succumb to the pressure to cheat. Drawing on an experience later in life, when he was in charge of a church youth group, Sproul continues:

I had about thirty young people in the class. On one occasion I said to them, "OK, let's get real honest here. How many of you ever cheat on tests?"

I was shocked by the response. Every hand in the room went up. I don't know if I was more shocked by the fact that they all did it or by the fact that they were all willing to admit it.

We then proceed to a lengthy discussion about *why* they cheated. The answers they gave included: "My parents put so much pressure on me to make good grades. . . ." "Everyone else is cheating and it is the only way I can compete." "I don't want to look stupid." "The tests aren't fair."

We talked it out. As a group we resolved to change our habits. For the entire semester I asked them each week: "Did you cheat this week?" Some of them stopped cheating immediately. Others struggled with it deeply. What emerged was a camaraderie

---

1. R. C. Sproul, *Pleasing God* (Wheaton, Ill.: Tyndale House Publishers, 1988), pp. 193–95.

among them whereby they were encouraging each other toward honesty.[2]

We encourage you to read this Living Insight with your teens and challenge them to be honest. It's better for them to have lower, honest grades than higher grades that are a lie.

2. Sproul, *Pleasing God*, pp. 195–96.

Chapter 12

SURVIVAL TRAINING FOR THE SCHOOL JUNGLE
Selected Scriptures

Every school year, a groggy army of children trudges through the misty dawn to the street corner and waits silently for a fleet of smoke-spewing buses to transport them into the education jungle. On the home front, parents worry about the spiritual and physical dangers their kids may encounter:

- Sex education courses that reduce moral standards to a matter of personal choice

- Self-esteem curriculum that borders on self-worship

- Stress reduction techniques that smack of New Age philosophy

- Literature textbooks that feature stories about the occult

- Social studies textbooks that promote "the new tolerance"

- Peer pressure

- Racial tensions, drugs, violence

How can a child survive and grow as a Christian in such an environment? Where can anxious parents find comfort? Thankfully, the Bible provides spiritual survival tips that reassure parents and prepare Christian young people to cut through the school jungle and emerge with stronger character.

The Biblical Picture

Let's begin this chapter by examining God's ideal learning environment: the home.

Idealistic Conception: The Home

After explaining God's commandments in detail, Moses told the Israelites to obey them in such a way that their children and grandchildren would also fear the Lord and keep His Law (Deut. 6:1–2). For Jewish families, school was always in session. The principal, Moses, gave his nation of parent-teachers these additional instructions:

99

"Hear, O Israel! The Lord is our God, the Lord is one! You shall love the Lord your God with all your heart and with all your soul and with all your might. These words, which I am commanding you today, shall be on your heart; and you shall teach them diligently to your sons and shall talk of them when you sit in your house and when you walk by the way and when you lie down and when you rise up." (vv. 4–7)

Devotion to the Lord was the goal; the Law was the curriculum; and any house, tree stump, or open road was the classroom. Children began their education at birth, and it lasted until they started their own families. According to God's plan, spiritual and secular training were integrated into one home-based educational system. To see the results, take a look at verse 24:

"So the Lord commanded us to observe all these statutes, to fear the Lord our God *for our good always and for our survival.*" (emphasis added)

But what if family structures start collapsing, as they have today? What if, because of outside demands, parents are unable to train their children at home?

Realistic Exceptions: The School

Many godly people thrived spiritually despite being deprived of God's ideal; notably Samuel, Daniel, and Moses himself were taught in schools outside the home. Let's observe their experiences so we can glean some helpful principles for school survival.

The boy Samuel. Samuel's mother, Hannah, had promised the Lord that if He would touch her barren womb and give her a son, she would dedicate him to His service (1 Sam. 1:1–11). The Lord answered her prayer, and she named her boy Samuel, which means "asked of the Lord" (see v. 20).

After she had weaned him, she honored her vow and handed her precious son over to the high priest, Eli. Resolutely, she told Eli:

"For this boy I prayed, and the Lord has given me my petition which I asked of Him. So I have also dedicated him to the Lord; as long as he lives he is dedicated to the Lord." And [Samuel] worshiped the Lord there. (vv. 27–28)

So Samuel's classroom was the temple, not the home. Our contemporary equivalent might be a Christian school. Certainly, such a safe environment would protect him from the world's influences, right? Perhaps not. Meet Samuel's peers—Eli's sons, Hophni and Phinehas:

> The sons of Eli were worthless men; they did not know the Lord. (2:12)

Not only were they unbelievers, they desecrated the Lord's temple by taking sacrificial meat from the people by force (vv. 15–17). They even had sexual relations "with the women who served at the doorway of the tent of meeting" (v. 22b). These were supposed to be Samuel's "spiritual" role models!

Amazingly, in spite of their influence, "the boy Samuel grew before the Lord" (v. 21b).

The teenager Daniel. The second young man who survived a hostile school environment was Daniel. He was only a teenager when the Babylonians—also known as the Chaldeans—conquered Jerusalem. After this devastating defeat, he was selected, along with several other promising young men, to move to Babylon and serve in King Nebuchadnezzar's court (Dan. 1:1–4).

When Daniel arrived, the king ordered a special diet for his body and special books for his mind. Whether he liked it or not, Daniel was enrolled in the Chaldean indoctrination program. The king required that he study Chaldean literature and language, and one commander also assigned Daniel a Chaldean name, Belteshazzar (see vv. 5–8).

Imagine young Daniel's situation. He is miles away from the nurturing environment of his home and family. Educated in what we could consider a military academy, he faces hostile forces that are designed to break down his religious and cultural convictions and make him a loyal Chaldean, inside and out.

But despite this pressure, Daniel held fast to his faith.

The young adult Moses. Our third example is Moses. Born during Pharaoh's terrifying decree to kill all Hebrew baby boys, he was placed by the Nile River in a basket, where Pharaoh's daughter discovered him and adopted him into the royal family (Exod. 2:1–10).

Not until we read the New Testament, though, does a window of information open concerning Moses' schooling. According to Stephen's speech in Acts 7,

"Moses was educated in all the learning of the Egyptians, and he was a man of power in words and deeds." (v. 22)

Our current counterpart of Moses' school would be a liberal university. The Greek word translated "learning" is *sophia*, "wisdom." At Egypt U., Moses was absorbing the same wisdom and know-how that built the pyramids. Theologian F. B. Meyer gives us a tour of Moses' alma mater:

> When old enough he was probably sent to be *educated in the college*, which had grown up around the Temple of the Sun, and has been called "the Oxford of Ancient Egypt." There he would learn to read and write the mysterious hieroglyph; there, too, he would be instructed in mathematics, astronomy, and chemistry, in all of which the Egyptians were adepts.[1]

In the university, Moses was taught to think, act, and worship like the Egyptians. Yet, in his heart, he remained true to the God of the Hebrews.

How did he stay faithful amidst such scholastic pressure? For that matter, how did the teenager Daniel thrive spiritually in his Babylonian military academy? And how did the boy Samuel avoid the mistakes of his rebellious peers in his "Christian school"?

Analytical Patterns

Let's return to each boy's story and analyze what helped them spiritually survive the school jungle.

Samuel: The Child in Christian School

Three factors can be seen in Samuel's situation. First, *there was the continued influence of a godly parent*. Every year, Hannah would make a new robe for Samuel and bring it to him in the temple (1 Sam. 2:18–19). Although she lived far away, he knew she was thinking about him and praying for him, for Hannah was a woman of prayer (see 1:9–18; 2:1–10). Hannah's godliness must have powerfully influenced her young son.

1. F. B. Meyer, *Moses: The Servant of God* (Grand Rapids, Mich.: Zondervan Publishing House, 1953), p. 21.

Second, *Samuel maintained balance.* According to 2:26, "the boy Samuel was growing in stature and in favor both with the Lord and with men." These words are said of only one other person in Scripture—Jesus Christ (Luke 2:52). Like young Jesus, Samuel modeled a genuineness that appealed equally to the Father and to other people. He didn't act one way with his friends and another way at "church." He was real.

Third, *Samuel's relationship with the Lord was vital.* Even though he lived with religion day after day, his zeal for the Lord remained fresh. As a result, "Samuel grew and the Lord was with him and let none of his words fail" (3:19).

Impersonal religiosity can dull a young person's appetite for the Lord. By helping children develop a direct relationship with God through prayer and Bible study, we can preserve their enthusiasm for a genuine spiritual life.

Daniel: The Teenager in Military Academy

What were Daniel's survival strategies? First, *he faced temptations with preestablished convictions.* According to Daniel 1:8a,

> Daniel made up his mind that he would not defile himself with the king's choice food or with the wine which he drank.

The key phrase, "made up his mind" can be translated literally as "lay to heart."[2] Daniel identified his convictions and weaved them together like the strands of a sturdy rope. Then he tied them to his heart, giving himself a strong hold on right and wrong before any grip-loosening situations came along.

Second, *he handled pressure with wisdom.* He didn't elbow his way to the front of the class and priggishly announce his standards; instead, he politely "sought permission from the commander of the officials that he might not defile himself" (v. 8b).

Third, *God honored his life with academic excellence.* Because Daniel and his friends maintained their integrity, "God gave them knowledge and intelligence in every branch of literature and wisdom" (v. 17a). A clear conscience frees teenagers to grow academically. God may not miraculously change all your grades to

---

2. William Gesenius, *A Hebrew and English Lexicon of the Old Testament,* trans. Edward Robinson, ed. Francis Brown, S. R. Driver, and Charles A. Briggs (Oxford, England: Clarendon Press, n.d.), p. 525.

103

A's, but He will honor you with something far more important: wisdom.

Moses: The Young Adult in the Liberal University

Finally, what were Moses' secrets of surviving the immoral influences of his university? First, *his faith was stronger than his feelings.* Underscoring this point, the author of Hebrews writes: "By faith Moses . . . refused to be called the son of Pharaoh's daughter" (11:24); "By faith he left Egypt" (v. 27); "By faith he kept the Passover" (v. 28); and "By faith they passed through the Red Sea" (v. 29).

Where did he acquire such strong faith? It must have been placed in his heart as a preschooler while he was still with his mother and father.[3]

Second, *his priorities determined his decisions.* The writer to the Hebrews also observes that Moses chose

> rather to endure ill-treatment with the people of God, than to enjoy the passing pleasures of sin, considering the reproach of Christ greater riches than the treasures of Egypt; for he was looking to the reward. (vv. 25–26)

By making the joys of heaven his number one priority and by carefully looking ahead to the consequences of his actions, he was able to accept hardship and say no to anything that would rob him of his reward.

From the vantage point of experience, parents can help their kids consider the consequences of their choices. Parents, don't be afraid to point out to your children life's potholes. When they get to college, they'll thank you for teaching them discernment.

Conclusion: Practical Principles

Wrapping up these truths, here are two final principles to slip into your survival pack.

First, a word to students—*no pressure is greater than God's power: draw upon it!* Although peer pressure is great, schools don't force

---

3. According to F. B. Meyer, Moses' mother was probably his nursemaid until he reached age four or five, long enough "to receive into his heart the love of the only God, which was to become the absorbing passion and pole-star of his career." *Moses: The Servant of God,* p. 20.

you to believe certain philosophies or attend certain parties. You make your own choices. When you're tempted, call upon God's power within you. "Greater is He who is in you than he who is in the world" (1 John 4:4b).

Second, to parents—*no school can fully erase the impact of a godly home: develop it!* We've now come full circle to God's ideal learning environment, the home. You still have the greatest influence in your children's lives, despite the persuasive power of school and friends. Keep on modeling holiness and teaching your children God's ways . . .

> "when you sit in your house and when you walk by the way and when you lie down and when you rise up." (Deut. 6:7b)

Living Insights

Are your school-age children developing the inner qualities necessary to survive in school? For a few moments, think about their character strengths and weaknesses in light of the characteristics we discussed in this lesson. In the following chart, fill in your children's names and mark *SG* if they are showing growth in that area, and *NI* if they need improvement.

Children's names:			
Genuineness			
Zeal for the Lord			
Commitment to preestab-lished convictions			
Humility and wisdom under pressure			
Faithfulness to God, regard-less of feelings			
Eternal priorities			

Certainly, no child—or adult—will excel in all of these areas all the time. Your children may be strong one day and weak the next. But now that you understand what characteristics to nurture, determine to praise your kids when they mature in these areas.

In the space provided, note a few of the ways your children have exhibited some of these qualities.

_____

_____

_____

What are two specific ways you can encourage and reward your children's improvement this week?

_____

_____

_____

Now return to the chart for a moment. How do *you* measure up to these character qualities? Pick one or two characteristics and jot down some ways you can model growth in these areas for your children.

_____

_____

_____

Living Insights STUDY TWO

The first things people usually see in our homes are the little treasures we display on a shelf or a table. Keepsakes such as a black-and-white photograph in an antique frame or a well-worn family Bible speak clearly about who we are and what we value.

As people enter our lives, they notice our character qualities in much the same way. Our honesty, compassion, genuineness, or patience are often the first things others see in us.

As we wrap up our study on biblical character, think back on the many qualities you've encountered. Which of these would you like to display more prominently in your life? Why?

Quality: _____ Reason:_____

_____

_____

Quality: _____ Reason:_____

_____

_____

Quality: _____ Reason:_____

_____

_____

Quality: _____ Reason:_____

_____

_____

The next time you notice the keepsakes in your home, think of the biblical character qualities you've displayed on the shelves of your life. Show them with confidence, for they reveal Christ's presence in you.

BOOKS FOR
PROBING FURTHER

The best way to see the true colors of a gem is to place it on black velvet and illuminate it with a piercing white light. In the same way, our true character is revealed when troubles cast their dark shadows across our souls and pressure's spotlight pierces our hearts.

Are you struggling through dark times right now? What character qualities are sparkling? Which seem to be a bit lackluster?

If you would like to polish up a few areas, the following list of sources will show you where to apply some elbow grease. Pick one or two that fit your situation, and be willing to let the Lord burnish your character into a rare and radiant diamond.

Canfield, Ken R. *The 7 Secrets of Effective Fathers*. Wheaton, Ill.: Tyndale House Publishers, 1992.

Cole, Edwin Louis. *Strong Men in Tough Times: Developing Strong Character in an Age of Compromise*. Altamonte, Fla.: Creation House, 1994.

Colson, Charles, with Ellen Santilli Vaughn. *The Body: Being Light in Darkness*. Dallas, Tex.: Word Publishing, 1992.

Eisenman, Tom L. *Temptations Men Face: Straightforward Talk on Power, Money, Affairs, Perfectionism, Insensitivity*. Downers Grove, Ill.: InterVarsity Press, 1992.

Evans, Debra. *Women of Character*. Grand Rapids, Mich.: Zondervan Publishing House, 1997.

Huggins, Kevin. *Parenting Adolescents*. Rev. ed. Colorado Springs, Colo.: NavPress, 1992.

Lewis, Robert and William Hendricks. *Rocking the Roles: Building a Win-Win Marriage*. Rev. ed. Colorado Springs, Colo.: NavPress, 1999.

Morley, Patrick M. *The Man in the Mirror: Solving the 24 Problems Men Face*. Grand Rapids, Mich.: Zondervan Publishing House, 1997.

Swindoll, Charles R. *The Quest for Character*. Portland, Oreg.: Multnomah Books, 1987; Grand Rapids, Mich.: Zondervan Publishing House, 1993.

White, Jerry. *Dangers Men Face: Overcoming the Five Greatest Threats to Living Well*. Colorado Springs, Colo.: NavPress, 1997.

White, Jerry. *Honesty, Morality, and Conscience*. Rev. ed. Colorado Springs, Colo.: NavPress, 1996.

Some of the books listed above may be out of print and available only through a library. For those currently available, please contact your local Christian bookstore. Books by Charles R. Swindoll are available through Insight for Living. IFL also offers some books by other authors—please note the ordering information that follows and contact the office that serves you.

NOTES

NOTES

NOTES

ORDERING INFORMATION

CHARACTER COUNTS

If you would like to order additional Bible study guides, purchase the audiocassette series that accompanies this guide, or request our product catalogs, please contact the office that serves you.

United States and International locations:

Insight for Living
Post Office Box 69000
Anaheim, CA 92817-0900

1-800-772-8888, 24 hours a day, seven days a week
(714) 575-5000, 8:00 A.M. to 4:30 P.M., Pacific time, Monday to Friday

Canada:

Insight for Living Ministries
Post Office Box 2510
Vancouver, BC, Canada V6B 3W7

1-800-663-7639, 24 hours a day, seven days a week
infocanada@insight.org

Australia:

Insight for Living, Inc.
20 Albert Street
Blackburn, VIC 3130, Australia

Toll-free 1800 772 888 or (03) 9877-4277, 8:30 A.M. to 5:00 P.M., Monday to Friday
iflaus@insight.org

World Wide Web:

www.insight.org

Study Guide Subscription Program

Bible study guide subscriptions are available. Please call or write the office nearest you to find out how you can receive our Bible study guides on a regular basis.